WILLIAMS-SONOMA

Classic Pasta at Home

GENERAL EDITOR
Chuck Williams

RECIPES
Janet Fletcher

PHOTOGRAPHY
Richard Eskite

TIME
LIFE
BOOKS

TIME-LIFE BOOKS
Time-Life Books is a division of Time Life Inc.
Time-Life is a trademark of Time Warner Inc. U.S.A

TIME-LIFE CUSTOM PUBLISHING
Vice President and Publisher: Terry Newell
Managing Editor: Donia Ann Steele
Director of New Product Development:
    Quentin McAndrew
Vice President of Sales and Marketing: Neil Levin
Director of Financial Operations: J. Brian Birky

WILLIAMS-SONOMA
Founder and Vice-Chairman: Chuck Williams
Book Buyer: Victoria Kalish

WELDON OWEN INC.
President: John Owen
Vice President and Publisher: Wendely Harvey
Chief Operating Officer: Larry Partington
Associate Publisher: Lisa Atwood
Project Coordinator: Judith Dunham
Consulting Editor: Norman Kolpas
Copy Editor: Sharon Silva
Design: Kari Perin, Perin+Perin
Production Director: Stephanie Sherman
Production Manager: Jen Dalton
Production Editor: Sarah Lemas
Vice President International Sales: Stuart Laurence
Co-editions Director: Derek Barton
Food Stylist: George Dolese
Prop Stylist: Sara Slavin
Photo Production Coordinator: Juliann Harvey
Photo Assistants: Lara Hata, Kevin Hossler
Food Styling Assistant: Jill Sorensen
Glossary Illustrations: Alice Harth

A NOTE ON WEIGHTS AND MEASURES
All recipes include customary U.S. and metric measurements. Metric conversions are based on a standard developed for these books and have been rounded off. Actual weights may vary.

The Williams-Sonoma Lifestyle Series
conceived and produced by Weldon Owen Inc.
814 Montgomery Street, San Francisco, CA 94133

In collaboration with Williams-Sonoma
3250 Van Ness Avenue, San Francisco, CA 94109

Separations by Colourscan Overseas Co. Pte. Ltd.
Printed in Singapore by Tien Wah Press (Pte.) Ltd.

A WELDON OWEN PRODUCTION
Copyright © 1998 Weldon Owen Inc.
All rights reserved, including the right of
reproduction in whole or in part in any form.

First printed in 1998
10 9 8 7 6 5 4 3 2

Library of Congress
Cataloging-in-Publication Data

Fletcher, Janet Kessel.
    Classic pasta at home / general editor, Chuck
Williams ; by Janet Fletcher ; photography by
Richard Eskite.
        p. cm. — (Williams-Sonoma lifestyles)
    Includes index.
    ISBN 0-7835-4610-6
    1. Cookery (Pasta) I. Title.   II. Series.
TX809.M17F5497 1998
641.8'22––dc21   97-28551
                                           CIP

A NOTE ON NUTRITIONAL ANALYSIS
Each recipe is analyzed for significant nutrients per serving. Not included in the analysis are ingredients that are optional or added to taste, or are suggested as an alternative or substitution either in the recipe or in the recipe introduction or accompanying tip. In recipes that yield a range of servings, the analysis is for the middle of that range.

Contents

Welcome

We've all gone mad for pasta lately, enjoying it often as a quick, easy, and satisfying main course. At the same time, countless new and unusual pasta recipes keep turning up in newspaper food sections and popular magazines to feed our growing interest.

I find, though, that I keep coming back to a handful of tried-and-true Italian recipes. And when I talk to other people who love good food, the pasta recipes they enjoy most are also those that have stood the test of time: the classics.

That, in a nutshell, is the reason behind this book. It includes 30 outstanding recipes for the kinds of main-course pastas you'll turn to time and time again, whether looking for a quick weeknight supper or something special for a casual dinner party. It also includes simple antipasti, salads, and desserts to help you round out your meal. You'll also find instructions on preparing and cooking dried, fresh, and filled pastas and on planning menus.

All I'd like to add is a single suggestion: Always assemble and prep your ingredients beforehand, so the recipes will come together quickly and smoothly. Then, get ready to enjoy some of the tastiest, most authentic pasta you've ever eaten.

Chuck Williams

Pleasures of Pasta

However elegant the meal, eating pasta adds a delightfully informal note. To pick up strands or ribbons, just snare a few with your fork and twirl them up while holding the tips of the tines against the edge of a shallow bowl or, if you need more help, against the hollow of a spoon.

Enjoying Classic Pasta

Like any creation labeled "classic," pasta dishes deserving of that adjective have a simplicity, a logic, and even a beauty that have helped them endure for centuries. Look at dishes like Linguine with Clams (page 75), or even humble Spaghetti and Meatballs (page 78). They offer you a taste of Italy's culinary history—and a good explanation of why that nation's cooking is so popular around the world.

Such pasta classics remain favorites largely because they are the kinds of dishes Italians—and countless fans of Italian food—enjoy in restaurants and love to cook and eat at home as well. That universal appeal continues to grow among those whose busy lives lead them to seek out food that is comforting and easy to prepare.

In fact, the very role pasta plays in home-style meals has changed. In Italy, it was once served almost exclusively as a starter or as a small dish between the first course, or antipasto, and the main course. Today, pasta has become a favorite main course in its own right.

Start with a simple appetizer or salad and finish with an equally uncomplicated dessert, and you have a homemade three-course meal that feels like a feast—even though it can usually be put together in minutes.

Saucing and Serving Pasta

The ease and speed with which you can cook pasta belie its incredible variety: Italians have invented literally hundreds of different shapes, along with endless ways to sauce and serve them. Yet, all pastas fall into two basic types: dried pasta, most commonly made with just flour and water, and fresh pasta, which is usually a combination of flour and eggs.

One type is not better than the other, however, as is too often assumed. Instead, each type has its own place in cooking. Fresh pastas have a soft, silken texture and a porous surface that generally work best with rich sauces containing butter, cream, or cheese. Resilient and chewy dried pasta is better suited to more robust sauces made with olive oil and tomatoes or a mixture of vegetables.

Pasta shapes, some common examples of which can be seen on page 10, also define the suitability of a sauce. Thin strands such as spaghettini, spaghetti, and linguine are best matched with more delicate, fluid sauces. Ribbons like fettuccine and tagliatelle hold heavier sauces better. And the curves and hollows of shapes such as rigatoni, farfalle, and orecchiette are designed to capture rustic, chunky sauces.

No matter what pasta recipe you choose, it is easy to present it at home in authentic style. Most Italians serve individual portions in broad, shallow bowls or large rimmed plates that help contain the sauce. It's up to you whether you bring the pasta to the table individually plated or in a large bowl for serving family-style.

In most cases, all that is needed for eating pasta properly is a table fork, which Italians use to snare a few strands at a time, twirling them around the tines held against the curved side of their bowl or plate.

Eating long strands of pasta can get a bit messy, but don't worry too much about decorum.

No less a figure of elegance than the famous Italian actress Sophia Loren reputedly once remarked, "Spaghetti can be eaten successfully if you inhale it like a vacuum cleaner."

Serving Wine with Pasta

Italians love wine with their meals, and most wouldn't dream of enjoying pasta without it. If you would like to serve wine, a few simple guidelines will help you make a good choice.

Select a wine with qualities that complement the sauce or filling. Generally, a crisp white, such as Pinot Grigio, Orvieto, or Verdicchio, goes well with pastas featuring vegetables, seafood, or chicken. If those dishes include tomatoes, however, a light red—Sangiovese or Valpolicella—could also be served.

Both white and red wines go well with rich cream and cheese sauces. Try a big, buttery Italian Chardonnay, a slightly fruity white Soave, or a fruity red such as Lambrusco. Robust reds are ideal partners for pastas tossed with hearty meat sauces; try a Chianti Classico, Barolo, or Barbaresco.

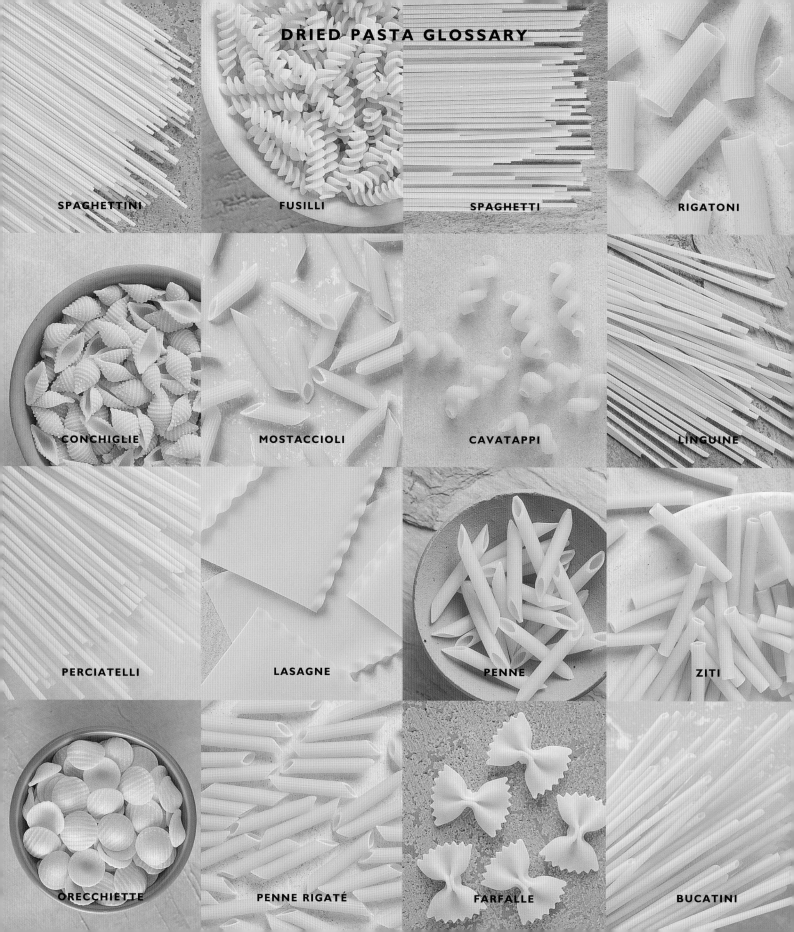

DRIED PASTA GLOSSARY

SPAGHETTINI

FUSILLI

SPAGHETTI

RIGATONI

CONCHIGLIE

MOSTACCIOLI

CAVATAPPI

LINGUINE

PERCIATELLI

LASAGNE

PENNE

ZITI

ORECCHIETTE

PENNE RIGATÉ

FARFALLE

BUCATINI

How to Cook and Sauce Pasta

Cooking and saucing pasta is simple. Use 5–6 quarts (5–6 l) boiling water for every 1 pound (500 g) of pasta, adding about 1 tablespoon salt to the water for seasoning. When the pasta is done, drain it briefly. Cooked pasta that is still slightly wet with cooking water combines more readily with sauce. If the sauce is too thick, add some reserved cooking water to thin it.

COOKING AND SAUCING

1. Bring a large pot three-fourths full of generously salted water to a rolling boil over high heat. Add the pasta—here, penne—and stir to prevent it from sticking together.

2. Cook the pasta until al dente (tender but firm to the bite). Place a colander in the sink and drain the pasta, reserving some of the cooking water.

3. While the pasta is still dripping slightly, combine it with the sauce. Here, the penne has been returned to its warm cooking pot and the sauce poured over it. Toss well, adding some of the reserved cooking liquid if the sauce is too thick.

Making Fresh Egg Pasta

1. Form a mound of flour, and then make a well with high, thick walls. Add eggs and, using a fork, gradually beat in the flour from the sides to form the dough.

2. When the dough is no longer wet, knead gently by hand on a lightly floured work surface for about 5 minutes, adding flour as needed until smooth and no longer sticky.

5. Starting at the second-to-widest setting, pass the dough through the rollers again. Continue, making the rollers narrower each time, until the dough reaches the desired thinness.

3. Working with half the dough, flatten with a rolling pin, flour lightly, and pass through the rollers of a pasta machine at the widest setting. Fold the resulting strip into thirds.

4. Using the rolling pin, flatten the dough until it is thin enough to pass through the rollers. Flour, roll, fold, and flatten at the widest setting 9 more times, making the dough smooth and supple.

Fresh Egg Pasta

2¼ cups (11½ oz/360 g) unbleached
  all-purpose (plain) flour, plus flour
  as needed
3 eggs, lightly beaten
semolina flour for dusting

❋ Place the 2¼ cups (11½ oz/360 g) flour in a mound on a work surface. Make a well in the center large enough to hold the eggs and pour the beaten eggs into the well. Using a fork, begin gradually incorporating some of the flour from the sides, taking care not to break the flour wall. When the eggs are no longer runny, you can stop worrying about the wall. Continue working in more flour until the dough is no longer wet.

❋ Begin kneading the dough by hand, adding as much additional all-purpose flour as needed until the dough is smooth and no longer sticky, 2–3 minutes. Scoop up any remaining flour and pass it through a sieve to remove any large particles. Set the sieved flour aside.

❋ Dust baking sheets with semolina flour. Divide the dough in half. Keep one-half on the work surface, covered with a kitchen towel to prevent it from drying. Set up your pasta machine alongside another work surface. Lightly flour the work surface with some of the reserved sieved flour. Using a rolling pin, flatten the other dough half into a rectangle thin enough to go through the rollers at the widest setting. Pass the dough through the rollers once, then lay the resulting ribbon down on the work surface and flour it lightly. Fold into thirds lengthwise to make a rectangle and flour both sides lightly. Flatten the dough with the rolling pin until it is thin enough to go through the rollers again. With one of the two open edges going first, pass the dough through the rollers nine more times at the widest setting; after each time, flour, fold, and flatten the dough as described. After 10 trips through the wide rollers, the dough should be completely smooth and supple.

❋ Now you are ready to thin the dough. Starting at the second-to-widest setting, pass the dough through the rollers repeatedly, setting the rollers one notch narrower each time. When the pasta ribbon gets unwieldy, cut it in half and continue rolling one part at a time until the dough reaches the desired thinness.

❋ Arrange the finished pasta sheets on the prepared baking sheets and cover with kitchen towels to prevent drying. Repeat the entire process with the second half of dough. Cut the pasta by hand or machine as desired.

MAKES 1 LB (500 G) DOUGH

FRESH SPINACH PASTA

Adding fresh spinach lends a chewier texture and greater flavor to classic egg pasta dough.

1 lb (500 g) fresh spinach, thick
  stems removed
2 eggs
about 3 cups (15 oz/470 g) unbleached
  all-purpose (plain) flour
semolina flour for dusting

❋ *Rinse the spinach well, drain briefly, and place the damp spinach in a large frying pan. Cover and cook over medium heat until the spinach wilts, 2–3 minutes. Drain in a sieve under cold running water. When cool, squeeze thoroughly dry.*

❋ *Place the spinach in a food processor with 1 of the eggs. Process to a smooth purée, stopping once or twice to scrape down the sides of the work bowl.*

❋ *Make the pasta dough as directed for Fresh Egg Pasta (at left), putting the spinach mixture and the remaining egg, lightly beaten, into the well of flour, and then gradually working in the flour to make a dough. When fully incorporated, knead and roll out the pasta dough as directed for Fresh Egg Pasta.*

MAKES 1½ LB (750 G) DOUGH

Shaping and Filling Fresh Pasta

Some of the best-loved classic pasta recipes are those in which fresh pasta dough is wrapped around a well-seasoned filling. While such recipes require extra effort, they are still easy, as you can see in these demonstrations for Butternut Squash Agnolotti (page 42), Cheese Ravioli (page 63), and Spinach Cannelloni (page 46). In fact, once you have mastered the basic technique, a sheet of fresh pasta can become the perfect canvas for a wide range of fillings and shapes.

When making filled pasta, a few simple precautions will help you get the best results. First, start with a good-quality dough, following the instructions on page 13 or buying fresh dough sheets from a pasta shop or Italian delicatessen. Try to work quickly and efficiently, preparing your filling first so that the pasta will stay soft and pliable. Brushing the edges of the dough with water will help the dough stick together, effectively sealing the filling inside.

The only other precaution is not to cook filled pasta vigorously. Bring the cooking water only to a gentle boil, so that its movement won't jostle the edges open.

AGNOLOTTI
On a semolina-dusted work surface, cut out circles of fresh pasta with a 3-inch (7.5-cm) cookie cutter. Place ½ teaspoon of filling—here, butternut squash—in the center of each. Lightly moisten the edges with water, fold in half, and press firmly to seal.

RAVIOLI

1. Place 1½ teaspoons filling at even intervals in a single row along one side of a pasta sheet. Lightly moisten the pasta around each mound of filling with water, then fold the pasta in half lengthwise to cover the mounds of filling.

2. Press down firmly between and around the filling to seal the pasta edges. With a fluted pastry wheel, cut between the mounds of filling into ravioli.

CANNELLONI

Cook 5- to 6-inch (13- to 15-cm) squares of pasta dough in boiling water for 10 seconds; cool in ice water with 1 tablespoon olive oil. Pat dry on a damp kitchen towel. Spread ¼ cup (2 oz/60 g) filling evenly over each square, then roll up into a log and finish as directed in recipe.

Planning Menus

The recipes in this book have been created to complement one another, offering you countless opportunities to mix and match them in menus to suit any occasion. Follow any of the 10 suggestions listed here, or use them as examples to inspire your own. When planning any pasta menu, think first about the kind of meal you are serving—casual or elegant, light or hearty—and then consider the likes and dislikes of your guests. Think, too, about the pacing of the meal, serving a simple first course, for example, before a rich and robust pasta. Let the best seasonal ingredients in your market help you reach the final decisions on what to prepare. And don't forget good, crusty bread to sop up the sauce.

Springtime Celebration

Bresaola with Asparagus Salad
PAGE 22

Farfalle with Peas and
Prosciutto
PAGE 81

Panna Cotta
with Strawberries
PAGE 101

Sicilian Supper

Baked Eggplant Rolls
PAGE 29

Spaghetti with Seafood
PAGE 72

Lemon Gelato
PAGE 98

From the Farmers' Market

Fava Bean and Pecorino Salad
PAGE 37

Fettuccine with Artichokes,
Prosciutto, and Cream
PAGE 71

Pears Poached
in Red Wine
PAGE 104

Family Dinner

Tossed Green Salad

Mushroom Lasagne
PAGE 77

Mixed Fruit Salad
PAGE 107

After-Work Supper

Roasted Peppers
with Anchovies
PAGE 21

Baked Mostaccioli
with Sausage and Eggplant
PAGE 55

Fresh Figs
or Seasonal Berries

Elegant Dinner Party

Baked Radicchio with
Prosciutto
PAGE 26

Fettuccine
with Three Cheeses
PAGE 38

Coffee Granita
PAGE 102

A Casual Meal

Warm Shrimp
and White Bean Salad
PAGE 34

Rigatoni with Sweet Peppers
PAGE 94

Fresh Pears or Peaches

Early Summer Repast

Tomato and Tuna Salad
PAGE 33

Pappardelle with Asparagus
PAGE 60

Panna Cotta
with Strawberries
PAGE 101

Seaside Supper

Arugula and Fennel Salad
with Shaved Parmesan
PAGE 30

Linguine with Clams
PAGE 75

Lemon Gelato
PAGE 98

After the Harvest

Swiss Chard
with Pine Nuts
PAGE 18

Butternut Squash Agnolotti
PAGE 42

Pears Poached
in Red Wine
PAGE 104

Swiss Chard with Pine Nuts

PREP TIME: 15 MINUTES

COOKING TIME: 15 MINUTES

INGREDIENTS

1 large bunch green Swiss chard, about 1¼ lb (625 g)

2 tablespoons extra-virgin olive oil

2 tablespoons pine nuts

2 cloves garlic, minced

salt to taste

COOKING TIP: This recipe can also be made with spinach leaves, which need only 3 minutes of cooking. For a sweet-sour accent, add about 1 tablespoon dried currants, plumped in warm water to cover for 20 minutes and drained, at the same time you season with the salt.

Serve this invitingly simple wilted salad before any pasta except one that includes leafy greens.

SERVES 4

❀ Trim the chard ribs from the leaves and wash separately. Drain the leaves in a colander. Cut the ribs into ½-inch (12-mm) pieces.

❀ Bring a pot three-fourths full of salted water to a boil. Add the ribs and cook until tender, 3–5 minutes. Drain.

❀ Meanwhile, put the leaves in a large frying pan with just the rinsing water clinging to them. Place over medium heat, cover, and cook, stirring once or twice, until they wilt, about 5 minutes. Uncover and continue to cook to evaporate any excess moisture. Stir in the ribs, then remove from the heat.

❀ In a small frying pan over medium-low heat, warm together the olive oil and pine nuts. Toast the nuts, stirring often, until golden brown, about 3 minutes. Stir in the garlic and cook 1 minute to release its fragrance.

❀ Add the garlic mixture to the chard, season with salt, and stir well to coat the chard evenly. Taste and add more salt if needed.

❀ Transfer to a serving dish. Let cool, then serve at room temperature.

NUTRITIONAL ANALYSIS PER SERVING: Calories 110 (Kilojoules 462); Protein 4 g; Carbohydrates 6 g; Total Fat 10 g; Saturated Fat 1 g; Cholesterol 0; Sodium 278 mg; Dietary Fiber 3 g

Roasted Peppers with Anchovies

PREP TIME: 20 MINUTES

COOKING TIME: 10 MINUTES

INGREDIENTS

6 large, thick-walled bell peppers
   (capsicums), preferably 2 each
   red, yellow, and green

2½ tablespoons extra-virgin olive oil

1½ tablespoons red wine vinegar,
   or to taste

1 large clove garlic, minced

1 can (2 oz/60 g) anchovy fillets in
   olive oil

salt to taste

2 tablespoons minced fresh flat-leaf
   (Italian) parsley

PREP TIP: When time is short, use
good-quality bottled roasted red
peppers for this recipe.

Canned anchovies vary greatly, and so does people's appreciation of them. Use as many fillets from the can as you like, or even all of them.

SERVES 4–6

❋ Preheat a broiler (griller). Cut the bell peppers in half lengthwise and remove the stems and seeds. Place, cut sides down, on a baking sheet. Broil (grill) until the skins blacken and blister. Remove from the broiler, drape the peppers loosely with aluminum foil, and let cool for 10 minutes, then peel away the skins. Cut lengthwise into strips ⅓ inch (9 mm) wide.

❋ Place the pepper strips in a large bowl. Add the olive oil, 1½ table-spoons wine vinegar, and garlic. Drain as many anchovy fillets as desired (see note) and finely mince them. Add to the pepper strips and season with salt. The peppers can be prepared up to this point several hours in advance and stored at room temperature.

❋ Stir in the parsley and adjust the seasonings just before serving, adding a splash more vinegar if needed.

NUTRITIONAL ANALYSIS PER SERVING: Calories 114 (Kilojoules 479); Protein 4 g; Carbohydrates 8 g; Total Fat 8 g; Saturated Fat 1 g; Cholesterol 5 mg; Sodium 333 mg; Dietary Fiber 2 g

Bresaola with Asparagus Salad

PREP TIME: 20 MINUTES

COOKING TIME: 2 MINUTES

INGREDIENTS

ice water

1 lb (500 g) tender asparagus tips, thinly sliced on the diagonal (about 2 lb/1 kg before trimming)

3½ tablespoons extra-virgin olive oil

2 tablespoons minced fresh flat-leaf (Italian) parsley

1 large shallot, minced

1 clove garlic, minced

salt and ground pepper to taste

lemon juice to taste

¼ lb (125 g) bresaola, sliced paper-thin (see note)

SERVING TIP: Scatter a few tissue-thin shavings of good-quality Parmesan cheese over each serving.

Save this antipasto for spring, when asparagus are at their best. If you can't find bresaola (cured air-dried beef), substitute prosciutto.

SERVES 4

❀ Have ready a bowl of ice water. Bring a pot three-fourths full of salted water to a boil. Add the asparagus and boil until tender-crisp, about 2 minutes. Drain and transfer to the ice water to stop the cooking. When cool, drain and pat dry with paper towels. Transfer to a bowl and add 2½ tablespoons of the olive oil and the parsley, shallot, and garlic. Season with salt, pepper, and lemon juice. Turn to coat the asparagus with the dressing.

❀ Divide the bresaola among individual plates, arranging the slices in a slightly overlapping ring. Put one-fourth of the asparagus salad in the center of each ring. Drizzle the bresaola lightly with the remaining 1 tablespoon olive oil and serve.

NUTRITIONAL ANALYSIS PER SERVING: Calories 199 (Kilojoules 836); Protein 12 g; Carbohydrates 5 g; Total Fat 16 g; Saturated Fat 3 g; Cholesterol 23 mg; Sodium 528 mg; Dietary Fiber 1 g

Artichokes, Roman Style

PREP TIME: 30 MINUTES

COOKING TIME: 35 MINUTES

INGREDIENTS

juice of 1 lemon

4 large artichokes

2 tablespoons chopped fresh flat-leaf
(Italian) parsley

2 tablespoons chopped fresh mint

2 cloves garlic, minced

4 tablespoons (2 fl oz/60 ml) olive oil

large pinch of salt, plus salt to taste

½ cup (4 fl oz/125 ml) dry white wine

½ cup (4 fl oz/125 ml) water

COOKING TIP: The outer leaves
removed from the artichokes can be
steamed and enjoyed on their own
with a dipping sauce of olive oil and
lemon juice.

Rome's Campo dei Fiori market offers some of the world's most beautiful artichokes, which are given the following treatment in countless Roman homes and restaurants.

SERVES 4

❀ Fill a bowl three-fourths full of water and add the lemon juice. Working with 1 artichoke at a time and starting at the base, break off about 3 or 4 rows of the tough outer leaves, snapping them downward, until you reach the pale yellow-green inner leaves, which are tender enough, when cooked, to eat in their entirety. Cut off about 1 inch (2.5 cm) from the top of the artichoke. Using a small, sharp knife, cut off the bottom of the stem and then peel the stem until it is a pale green. Trim away any tough green parts from the base. Drop the trimmed artichoke into the lemon water to prevent browning, and put an inverted plate in the bowl to keep it submerged. Repeat with the remaining artichokes.

❀ In a small bowl, combine the parsley, mint, garlic, 2 tablespoons of the olive oil, and large pinch of salt and stir to mix well.

❀ One at a time, remove the artichokes from the lemon water and, using your fingertips, gently open them slightly (like a flower) to expose the choke. Again using your fingers, pull out the prickly inner leaves and discard. Using a sharp-edged spoon, scoop out and discard the hairy chokes. Spoon one-fourth of the herb mixture into each artichoke cavity.

❀ In a 4-qt (2-l) saucepan over medium heat, warm the remaining 2 tablespoons olive oil. Add the artichokes, stem ends up, and then add the wine and water. Bring to a simmer, cover, and adjust the heat to maintain a gentle simmer. Cook until the artichoke bottoms are tender when pierced, about 30 minutes.

❀ Transfer the artichokes to a platter, stem ends up. Taste the cooking liquid; add salt if needed, then reduce over medium-high heat to about ¼ cup (2 fl oz/60 ml). Spoon over the artichokes. Serve warm (not hot) or at room temperature.

NUTRITIONAL ANALYSIS PER SERVING: Calories 200 (Kilojoules 840); Protein 5 g; Carbohydrates 18 g; Total Fat 14 g; Saturated Fat 2 g; Cholesterol 0; Sodium 198 mg; Dietary Fiber 9 g

Baked Radicchio with Prosciutto

PREP TIME: 10 MINUTES

COOKING TIME: 14 MINUTES

INGREDIENTS

2 heads radicchio, about ¾ lb (375 g) each

2 tablespoons olive oil

12 large, thin slices prosciutto

lemon wedges

PREP TIP: Belgian endive (chicory/witloof) can be substituted for the radicchio. Use 3 small-to-medium heads of endive for each head of radicchio, cutting each endive head in half lengthwise.

Accompany this warm and rustic antipasto with a chilled white wine. Scatter a few olives alongside each serving, if you like.

SERVES 6

❊ Preheat an oven to 400°F (200°C). Oil a baking sheet.

❊ Cut each radicchio head into 6 wedges through the stem end. Brush each wedge lightly with the olive oil. Wrap each wedge with a slice of prosciutto, then arrange on the prepared baking sheet and turn to coat the prosciutto with the oil.

❊ Bake until the radicchio is tender and the prosciutto begins to crisp, 12–14 minutes. Transfer to a platter and serve with lemon wedges.

NUTRITIONAL ANALYSIS PER SERVING: Calories 140 (Kilojoules 588); Protein 10 g; Carbohydrates 7 g; Total Fat 10 g; Saturated Fat 2 g; Cholesterol 23 mg; Sodium 549 mg; Dietary Fiber 1 g

Baked Eggplant Rolls

PREP TIME: 45 MINUTES, PLUS
2 HOURS FOR DRAINING

COOKING TIME: 1¼ HOURS

INGREDIENTS

2 eggplants (aubergines), about 1 lb
(500 g) each

1½ teaspoons salt, plus salt to taste

2 red bell peppers (capsicums)

¼ cup (1 oz/30 g) lightly toasted fine
fresh bread crumbs (see glossary,
page 108)

¾ cup (3 oz/90 g) grated pecorino
cheese

1 tablespoon pine nuts

4 tablespoons (2 fl oz/60 ml) extra-
virgin olive oil

2 cloves garlic, minced

ground pepper to taste

about 16 fresh basil leaves

white wine vinegar to taste

1 tablespoon minced fresh flat-leaf
(Italian) parsley

These tender eggplant rolls have a savory stuffing of bell pepper, pecorino cheese, and bread crumbs. Serve them before a pasta with tomato sauce.

MAKES 8 ROLLS; SERVES 4

✳ Trim the eggplants, then cut lengthwise into slices ⅓ inch (9 mm) thick. You should have 10–12 slices. Use only the 8 largest slices (reserve the others for another use). Arrange them on a rack. Using the 1½ teaspoons salt, sprinkle the tops of the slices. Let stand for 2 hours. The slices will exude moisture. Pat dry with paper towels.

✳ Bring a large pot three-fourths full of salted water to a boil. Working in batches, add the eggplant slices and cook until supple enough to roll easily, 5–6 minutes. Using tongs, transfer to a kitchen towel to drain.

✳ Meanwhile, preheat a broiler (griller). Cut the bell peppers in half lengthwise and remove the seeds. Place, cut sides down, on a baking sheet. Broil (grill) until the skins blacken and blister. Remove from the broiler, drape the peppers loosely with aluminum foil, and let cool for 10 minutes. Peel away the skins and chop the peppers finely.

✳ In a small bowl, combine the bell peppers, bread crumbs, ¼ cup (1 oz/30 g) of the pecorino cheese, pine nuts, and 1 tablespoon of the olive oil. Stir to mix well. In a small frying pan over medium-low heat, warm 1 tablespoon of the remaining olive oil. Add the garlic and sauté for 1 minute. Add to the bell pepper mixture. Season generously with salt and pepper.

✳ Preheat an oven to 375°F (190°C). Oil a baking dish large enough to accommodate the eggplant rolls in a single layer.

✳ Arrange the eggplant slices on a work surface. Divide the bread crumb stuffing evenly among the slices, spreading it in a thin layer. Tear the basil leaves into small pieces and scatter evenly over the stuffing. Roll up each slice into a neat cylinder, then arrange, seam sides down, in the prepared dish. Drizzle the rolls evenly with the remaining 2 tablespoons olive oil, and sprinkle lightly with vinegar.

✳ Bake until the eggplant is completely tender when pierced, about 1 hour. Remove from the oven and sprinkle evenly with the remaining ½ cup (2 oz/60 g) pecorino cheese and with the parsley. Serve hot or warm.

NUTRITIONAL ANALYSIS PER SERVING: Calories 298 (Kilojoules 1,252); Protein 8 g; Carbohydrates 17 g; Total Fat 23 g; Saturated Fat 7 g; Cholesterol 21 mg; Sodium 695 mg; Dietary Fiber 4 g

Arugula and Fennel Salad with Shaved Parmesan

PREP TIME: 15 MINUTES

INGREDIENTS

1 fennel bulb

½ lb (250 g) young arugula (rocket), thick stems removed

FOR THE DRESSING

3 tablespoons extra-virgin olive oil

1½ tablespoons lemon juice, or more to taste

1 shallot, minced

salt and ground pepper to taste

2 oz (60 g) Parmesan cheese

PREP TIP: If you like, omit the Parmesan and add segments from 2 navel oranges or blood oranges. Using a sharp knife, cut off all the citrus peel to reveal the flesh. Then carefully cut on both sides of each segment to free it from the membrane.

Nutty arugula and crisp, licorice-flavored fennel have a natural affinity that is highlighted in this salad with a brisk lemon dressing.

SERVES 6

❁ Cut off the stems and feathery tops and any bruised outer stalks from the fennel bulb. Halve the bulb lengthwise and cut away the core. Thinly slice the bulb crosswise and place in a large bowl with the arugula.

❁ To make the dressing, in a small bowl, whisk together the olive oil, 1½ tablespoons lemon juice, and shallot. Season with salt and pepper. Add the dressing to the arugula and fennel and toss to coat. Taste and adjust the seasonings, adding more lemon juice if needed.

❁ Divide the salad among individual plates. Using a vegetable peeler, shave about 4 paper-thin slices of Parmesan cheese onto each salad.

NUTRITIONAL ANALYSIS PER SERVING: Calories 117 (Kilojoules 491); Protein 5 g; Carbohydrates 3 g; Total Fat 10 g; Saturated Fat 3 g; Cholesterol 7 mg; Sodium 243 mg; Dietary Fiber 1 g

Tomato and Tuna Salad

PREP TIME: 20 MINUTES

INGREDIENTS

2 large tomatoes, seeded and
  chopped

½ lb (250 g) good-quality canned
  tuna (see note), drained and
  separated into large flakes

¼ cup (2 fl oz/60 ml) extra-virgin
  olive oil

¼ cup (1½ oz/45 g) minced red
  (Spanish) onion

2 teaspoons capers

2 cloves garlic, minced

salt to taste

white wine vinegar to taste

about 12 fresh basil leaves, torn into
  small pieces

1 heart butter (Boston) lettuce,
  separated into leaves

2 hard-boiled eggs, peeled and
  quartered lengthwise

12 Mediterranean-style oil-cured
  black olives

In summer, a cool, fresh salad of ripe tomatoes, hard-boiled eggs, and tuna makes an easy start to a pasta dinner. If you can find it, use good-quality Italian tuna packed in olive oil.

SERVES 4

❀ In a bowl, combine the tomatoes, tuna, olive oil, onion, capers, and garlic. Toss to mix. Season with salt and vinegar and toss again. Just before serving, stir in the basil.

❀ Arrange 2 or 3 lettuce leaves on each plate. Top each lettuce bed with one-fourth of the tomato-tuna mixture. Surround with the hard-boiled egg wedges and olives, dividing them evenly. Serve at once.

NUTRITIONAL ANALYSIS PER SERVING: Calories 295 (Kilojoules 1,239); Protein 20 g; Carbohydrates 8 g; Total Fat 21 g; Saturated Fat 4 g; Cholesterol 130 mg; Sodium 566 mg; Dietary Fiber 2 g

Warm Shrimp and White Bean Salad

PREP TIME: 20 MINUTES, PLUS
8 HOURS FOR SOAKING

COOKING TIME: 1¼ HOURS

INGREDIENTS

1⅛ cups (8 oz/250 g) dried large
white beans

6 cups (48 fl oz/1.5 l) water

½ yellow onion

1 fresh rosemary sprig, 4 inches
(10 cm) long

salt and ground pepper to taste

18 large shrimp (prawns), peeled

⅓ cup (3 fl oz/80 ml) extra-virgin
olive oil

⅓ cup (2 oz/60 g) minced red
(Spanish) onion

¼ cup (⅓ oz/10 g) minced fresh
flat-leaf (Italian) parsley

2 cloves garlic, minced

1 tablespoon red wine vinegar

Bright pink-and-white butterflied shrimp look beautiful against a background of plump white beans. Use dried beans that are less than a year old, or they will not cook evenly.

SERVES 6

❀ Pick over the beans and discard any misshapen beans or impurities. Rinse the beans and drain. Place in a bowl, add plenty of water to cover, and let soak for 8 hours. Drain the beans and place in a saucepan with the 6 cups (48 fl oz/1.5 l) water. Add the yellow onion and rosemary. Bring to a simmer over medium heat, skimming off any foam. Cover partially, adjust the heat to maintain a gentle simmer, and cook until the beans are tender, about 1 hour. Remove from the heat and remove the onion and woody rosemary sprig (leave any detached leaves). Season the beans generously with salt and pepper. Keep warm.

❀ Bring a large pot three-fourths full of salted water to a boil. Meanwhile, using a small knife, make a deep slit along the back of each peeled shrimp so it will open like a butterfly when cooked. With the tip of the knife or your fingers, lift up and pull out the long, veinlike intestinal tract. Add the shrimp to the boiling water and cook just until they turn pink, about 45 seconds; do not overcook. Drain and transfer to a large, shallow serving bowl.

❀ Drain the warm beans and add to the bowl along with the olive oil, red onion, parsley, garlic, and vinegar. Toss well. Taste and adjust the seasonings. Serve at once.

NUTRITIONAL ANALYSIS PER SERVING: Calories 271 (Kilojoules 1,138); Protein 15 g; Carbohydrates 25 g; Total Fat 13 g; Saturated Fat 2 g; Cholesterol 46 mg; Sodium 52 mg; Dietary Fiber 4 g

Fava Bean and Pecorino Salad

PREP TIME: 40 MINUTES

COOKING TIME: 2 MINUTES

INGREDIENTS

4 lb (2 kg) fava (broad) beans

ice water

2½–3 tablespoons extra-virgin
olive oil

2 tablespoons minced green (spring)
onion, including tender green tops

salt and ground pepper to taste

lemon juice to taste

8–12 soft lettuce leaves, preferably
red

2 oz (60 g) young pecorino cheese
such as Toscanello or Manchego

Tender spring fava beans are prized in southern Italy, where they are often eaten raw with young pecorino cheese. Here, this pleasing pairing is turned into a delicate salad with the addition of leaf lettuce, olive oil, and lemon juice.

SERVES 4

❁ Shell the fava beans. Have ready a bowl of ice water. Bring a pot three-fourths full of water to a boil. Add the favas and boil for 2 minutes, then drain. Transfer to the bowl of ice water to stop the cooking, then drain. Peel by pinching one end of each bean; it will slip easily from the skin.

❁ In a bowl, mix together the beans, olive oil to taste, and green onion. Season with salt, pepper, and lemon juice. Tear the lettuce into bite-sized pieces and add to the bowl. Toss gently. Using a vegetable peeler, shave the cheese into paper-thin slices directly into the bowl. Toss gently. Taste and adjust the seasonings. Transfer to a serving platter.

NUTRITIONAL ANALYSIS PER SERVING: Calories 255 (Kilojoules 1,071); Protein 12 g; Carbohydrates 19 g; Total Fat 15 g; Saturated Fat 4 g; Cholesterol 14 mg; Sodium 335 mg; Dietary Fiber 7

Fettuccine with Three Cheeses

PREP TIME: 15 MINUTES,
   PLUS 1 HOUR IF MAKING
   FRESH PASTA

COOKING TIME: 5 MINUTES

INGREDIENTS

1 cup (8 fl oz/250 ml) heavy (double) cream

1 cup (8 fl oz/250 ml) chicken broth

3 oz (90 g) Val d'Aosta fontina cheese, grated

2 oz (60 g) Gorgonzola dolcelatte cheese

½ cup (2 oz/60 g) grated Parmesan cheese

½ teaspoon coarsely cracked pepper, plus pepper to taste

salt to taste

1 lb (500 g) fresh fettuccine, home-made (page 13) or store-bought

2 tablespoons minced fresh flat-leaf (Italian) parsley

In this recipe, the partially cooked pasta finishes cooking in the creamy sauce, so it absorbs the sauce better. Serve this rich dish in small portions before a light main course, or as a main course with a crisp green salad.

SERVES 4–6

❀ Bring a large pot three-fourths full of salted water to a boil over high heat.

❀ While the water is heating, combine the cream and broth in a large, nonstick frying pan. Bring to a simmer over medium heat and simmer until slightly thickened, about 1½ minutes. Reduce the heat to low. Using a wooden spoon, stir in the fontina, Gorgonzola, and Parmesan cheeses until they melt. Add the ½ teaspoon pepper and season with salt. The sauce should seem thin at this point. Keep warm over low heat.

❀ Add the pasta to the boiling water and cook until slightly underdone, about 1 minute. Drain and transfer to the frying pan holding the sauce. Raise the heat to medium-high and simmer, stirring, until the pasta has absorbed most of the sauce, about 1 minute or less. It should be neither soupy nor gummy. Divide among warmed dishes. Top with a little more pepper and with the parsley, dividing it evenly. Serve at once.

NUTRITIONAL ANALYSIS PER SERVING: Calories 619 (Kilojoules 2,600); Protein 23 g; Carbohydrates 55 g; Total Fat 33 g; Saturated Fat 20 g; Cholesterol 230 mg; Sodium 1,042 mg; Dietary Fiber 2 g

Penne with Spicy Tomato Sauce

PREP TIME: 20 MINUTES

COOKING TIME: 30 MINUTES

INGREDIENTS

¼ cup (2 fl oz/60 ml) olive oil

4 cloves garlic, minced

¼–½ teaspoon red pepper flakes

2 tablespoons minced fresh flat-leaf (Italian) parsley

1½ lb (750 g) ripe plum (Roma) tomatoes, peeled, seeded, and chopped

salt to taste

1 lb (500 g) dried penne

½ cup (2 oz/60 g) grated pecorino cheese

PREP TIP: In cool-weather months, use 2 cups (12 oz/375 g) chopped canned plum (Roma) tomatoes instead of fresh ones. If necessary, simmer the sauce a few minutes longer to reduce it to the desired consistency.

The red pepper flakes make this sauce "angry" (arrabbiata) and give this dish its Italian name, penne all'arrabbiata. Use the lesser amount if your palate is timid, the greater amount if you prefer to taste the sauce the way it would likely be made in Rome.

SERVES 4–6

❀ In a large sauté pan over medium heat, warm the olive oil. Add the garlic and red pepper flakes (see note) and sauté for 1 minute to release the garlic's fragrance. Add 1 tablespoon of the parsley and cook for a few seconds, then add the tomatoes. Raise the heat to medium-high and simmer briskly, stirring often, until the tomatoes break down and form a sauce, about 15 minutes. Add water as necessary to thin the sauce and keep it from sticking. Season with salt. Remove from the heat.

❀ Bring a large pot three-fourths full of salted water to a boil over high heat. Add the pasta, stir well, and cook until al dente (tender but firm to the bite), about 12 minutes or according to the package directions. While the pasta is cooking, reheat the sauce gently over low heat.

❀ Drain the pasta, reserving about ½ cup (4 fl oz/125 ml) of the cooking water. Return the pasta to the warm pot. Add the sauce and toss. Add ¼ cup (1 oz/30 g) of the pecorino cheese and toss again, adding some of the reserved water if needed to thin the sauce. Divide among warmed dishes. Top each portion with one-fourth of the remaining ¼ cup (1 oz/30 g) cheese and the remaining 1 tablespoon parsley. Serve at once.

NUTRITIONAL ANALYSIS PER SERVING: Calories 508 (Kilojoules 2,134); Protein 15 g; Carbohydrates 75 g; Total Fat 16 g; Saturated Fat 4 g; Cholesterol 11 mg; Sodium 571 mg; Dietary Fiber 4 g

Butternut Squash Agnolotti with Butter and Sage

**PREP TIME: 1 HOUR, PLUS
1 HOUR FOR MAKING PASTA**

COOKING TIME: 50 MINUTES

INGREDIENTS

FOR THE FILLING

1 small butternut squash, about 1½ lb (750 g)

¼ cup (2 fl oz/60 ml) water

1 egg

¼ cup (1 oz/30 g) lightly toasted fine fresh bread crumbs (*see glossary, page 108*)

⅓ cup (1½ oz/45 g) grated Parmesan cheese

salt to taste

freshly grated nutmeg to taste

semolina flour for dusting

Fresh Egg Pasta (*page 13*)

2 tablespoons unsalted butter

2 tablespoons olive oil

36 large fresh sage leaves

salt and ground pepper to taste

1 cup (4 oz/120 g) grated Parmesan cheese

COOKING TIP: If you use a butternut squash that yields more than the amount of purée needed for the agnolotti filling, you can reheat it the next day with butter, salt, and pepper.

Use a fluted cookie cutter to make these irresistible agnolotti, pasta half-moons stuffed with creamy butternut squash.

SERVES 6

❀ To make the filling, preheat an oven to 375°F (190°C). Cut the squash in half lengthwise; scoop out and discard the seeds and strings. Cut each half into 10–12 chunks. Place in a baking dish in a single layer. Add the water; cover tightly with aluminum foil. Bake until the squash is tender when pierced, about 40 minutes. Let cool, then spoon the flesh from the skin into a food processor. Purée until smooth. Transfer 1 cup (8 fl oz/250 ml) purée to a bowl along with the egg, bread crumbs, and cheese. Stir well and season with salt and nutmeg. Cover and refrigerate until needed.

❀ Heavily dust 2 baking sheets with semolina flour. Following the directions on page 12, roll out the pasta dough to form the thinnest possible sheets. Working with 1 sheet at a time, place on a work surface dusted with semolina flour. Using a round, fluted 3-inch (7.5-cm) cookie cutter, cut out as many rounds as possible. Put ½ teaspoon of the squash filling in the center of each round, moisten the edges lightly with water, then fold in half and press firmly to seal. Transfer to the prepared baking sheets. Let dry for 30 minutes at room temperature. (If you let them stand longer, cover with a kitchen towel to prevent further drying.)

❀ Bring a large pot three-fourths full of salted water to a boil over high heat. Meanwhile, in a large sauté pan over medium heat, melt the butter with the olive oil. Add the sage leaves, reduce the heat to low, and cook, turning each leaf once, until they begin to crisp, 7–8 minutes. Transfer to paper towels to drain. Reserve the oil and butter in the pan.

❀ Add the agnolotti to the boiling water, stir gently, and cook at a gentle boil until al dente (tender but firm to the bite), about 2 minutes. Using a large sieve, transfer the agnolotti to a warmed serving bowl. Add the reserved oil and butter; season with salt and pepper, then toss gently to coat with the seasonings. Add ½ cup (2 oz/60 g) of the Parmesan cheese and the sage leaves and toss again. Serve at once. Pass the remaining ½ cup (2 oz/60 g) Parmesan cheese at the table.

NUTRITIONAL ANALYSIS PER SERVING: Calories 473 (Kilojoules 1,987); Protein 21 g; Carbohydrates 54 g; Total Fat 19 g; Saturated Fat 8 g; Cholesterol 170 mg; Sodium 740 mg; Dietary Fiber 3 g

Penne with Swordfish, Tomatoes, Olives, and Capers

PREP TIME: 40 MINUTES

COOKING TIME: 40 MINUTES

INGREDIENTS

¼ cup (2 fl oz/60 ml) olive oil

3 cloves garlic, minced

⅛ teaspoon red pepper flakes

1 lb (500 g) ripe plum (Roma) tomatoes, peeled, seeded, and diced

2 teaspoons minced fresh oregano

½ cup (4 fl oz/125 ml) water

salt to taste

¾ lb (375 g) swordfish fillets, any skin removed, cut into ½-inch (12-mm) dice

16 Kalamata olives or other Mediterranean brine-cured olives, pitted and quartered

1 tablespoon capers, rinsed and coarsely chopped if large

2 tablespoons minced fresh flat-leaf (Italian) parsley

1 lb (500 g) dried penne or spaghetti

PREP TIP: To speed preparation, look for jars of pitted Kalamata olives in well-stocked markets and in delicatessens specializing in Mediterranean foods.

This seafood sauce hails from Sicily, which boasts some of the world's finest swordfish. Like most fish and shellfish sauces for pasta, it does not need cheese.

SERVES 4–6

❁ In a large sauté pan over medium heat, warm the olive oil. Add the garlic and red pepper flakes and sauté for 1 minute to release the garlic's fragrance. Add the tomatoes, oregano, and water. Raise the heat to medium-high, bring to a simmer, and cook, stirring often, until the tomatoes break down and form a sauce, about 15 minutes. Season with salt. Reduce the heat, add the swordfish, cover, and simmer gently until the fish is opaque throughout, about 10 minutes.

❁ Using a wooden spoon, mash the swordfish into the sauce, breaking it up until no large pieces remain. Stir in the olives, capers, and 1 tablespoon of the parsley. Remove from the heat.

❁ Bring a large pot three-fourths full of salted water to a boil over high heat. Add the pasta, stir well, and cook until al dente (tender but firm to the bite), about 12 minutes or according to the package directions. While the pasta is cooking, reheat the sauce gently over low heat.

❁ Drain the pasta and return to the warm pot. Add the sauce and toss. Divide among warmed dishes. Top with the remaining 1 tablespoon parsley, dividing it evenly. Serve at once.

NUTRITIONAL ANALYSIS PER SERVING: Calories 588 (Kilojoules 2,470); Protein 26 g; Carbohydrates 75 g; Total Fat 20 g; Saturated Fat 3 g; Cholesterol 27 mg; Sodium 754 mg; Dietary Fiber 3 g

Spinach Cannelloni

PREP TIME: 1½ HOURS, PLUS
    1¼ HOURS FOR MAKING
    PASTA

COOKING TIME: 1¼ HOURS

INGREDIENTS

14–16 oz (440–500 g) fresh spinach
    leaves, stemmed

½ lb (250 g) whole-milk ricotta cheese

½ lb (250 g) whole-milk mozzarella
    cheese, shredded

1 egg

4 cloves garlic, minced

1 tablespoon minced fresh basil, plus
    8 basil leaves, torn into pieces

1 teaspoon salt, plus salt to taste

ground pepper to taste

semolina flour for dusting

¾ lb (375 g) Fresh Spinach Pasta
    (page 13)

1½ tablespoons unsalted butter

1½ tablespoons unbleached
    all-purpose (plain) flour

1 cup (8 fl oz/250 ml) milk

1 bay leaf

1 fresh thyme sprig

freshly grated nutmeg to taste

3 tablespoons olive oil

pinch of red pepper flakes

1 can (14½ oz/455 g) whole plum
    (Roma) tomatoes, chopped

ice water

½ cup (2 oz/60 g) grated Parmesan
    cheese

Cannelloni make an impressive party dish. You can assemble them 4 hours ahead and bake them just before serving.

SERVES 4–6

❋ Wash the spinach and place in a frying pan with the rinsing water clinging to the leaves. Cover and cook over medium heat until wilted, about 3 minutes. Rinse with cold running water. Squeeze dry and chop finely. In a bowl, combine the spinach, ricotta and mozzarella cheeses, egg, half of the garlic, and minced basil. Season with the 1 teaspoon salt and pepper to taste. Cover and refrigerate until needed.

❋ Dust 3 baking sheets with semolina flour. Following the directions on page 12, roll out the dough on a pasta machine to make thin sheets. Cut into 5- to 6-inch (13- to 15-cm) squares. Arrange on the prepared sheets. Cover with kitchen towels.

❋ Melt the butter in a saucepan over medium heat. Whisk in the flour. Cook, whisking constantly, for 1 minute. Add the milk and bring to a simmer, whisking constantly. Add the bay leaf and thyme, and season with nutmeg, salt, and pepper. Cook gently over low heat, whisking often, for about 20 minutes. Press the béchamel sauce through a coarse-mesh sieve into a bowl. In a sauté pan over medium heat, warm 2 tablespoons of the olive oil. Add the remaining garlic and the red pepper flakes and sauté for 1 minute. Add the tomatoes and salt to taste. Simmer, uncovered, for about 15 minutes. Pass the sauce through a food mill or purée in a food processor. Return to the sauté pan along with the basil leaves and simmer for 5 minutes.

❋ Preheat an oven to 400°F (200°C). Butter a 9-by-13-inch (23-by-33-cm) baking dish. Fill a large bowl with ice water and add the remaining 1 tablespoon olive oil. Bring a large pot three-fourths full of salted water to a boil. Cook the pasta squares, 2 sheets at a time, for 10 seconds only. Transfer to the ice water and unfurl the squares in the water, then lay flat on a damp kitchen towel and pat dry.

❋ Spread a scant ¼ cup (2 oz/60 g) spinach filling on each pasta square. Roll into a log, then place in the prepared dish. Top with the béchamel sauce, then with the tomato sauce. Sprinkle with the Parmesan. Bake, uncovered, until bubbling hot, about 20 minutes. Serve at once.

NUTRITIONAL ANALYSIS PER SERVING: Calories 645 (Kilojoules 2,709); Protein 31 g; Carbohydrates 53 g; Total Fat 35 g; Saturated Fat 17 g; Cholesterol 167 mg; Sodium 1,309 mg; Dietary Fiber 4 g

Linguine alla Carbonara

PREP TIME: 20 MINUTES

COOKING TIME: 10 MINUTES

INGREDIENTS

4 eggs

¾ cup (3 oz/90 g) grated Parmesan
   cheese

2 tablespoons minced fresh flat-leaf
   (Italian) parsley

1 teaspoon coarsely cracked pepper

½ teaspoon salt

1 lb (500 g) dried linguine

1 tablespoon olive oil

1 tablespoon unsalted butter

¼ lb (125 g) pancetta, coarsely
   chopped

2 cloves garlic, minced

Be sure to serve this classic Roman pasta on warmed dishes to keep it warm longer. The heat of the pasta partially cooks the eggs. Note, however, that many health professionals advise against serving eggs that are not fully cooked to infants, the elderly, or anyone with a compromised immune system.

SERVES 4–6

❋ In a large bowl, combine the eggs, Parmesan cheese, parsley, pepper, and salt. Whisk to blend.

❋ Bring a large pot three-fourths full of salted water to a boil over high heat. Add the pasta, stir well, and cook until al dente (tender but firm to the bite), about 10 minutes or according to the package directions.

❋ While the pasta is cooking, combine the olive oil, butter, pancetta, and garlic in a sauté pan over medium heat and cook, stirring occasionally, until the pancetta renders some of its fat, about 3 minutes; do not let it become crisp. Keep warm over low heat.

❋ Using tongs, transfer the pasta, still dripping wet, to the bowl with the egg mixture. Toss immediately to coat with egg. Add the contents of the sauté pan and continue tossing until the egg coats the pasta evenly in a creamy sauce. Add a little of the pasta cooking water if needed to thin the sauce. Divide among warmed dishes. Serve at once.

NUTRITIONAL ANALYSIS PER SERVING: Calories 592 (Kilojoules 2,486); Protein 26 g; Carbohydrates 70 g; Total Fat 22 g; Saturated Fat 9 g; Cholesterol 201 mg; Sodium 1,097 mg; Dietary Fiber 2 g

Penne alla Puttanesca

PREP TIME: 30 MINUTES

COOKING TIME: 30 MINUTES

INGREDIENTS

¼ cup (2 fl oz/60 ml) olive oil

4 cloves garlic, minced

1 tablespoon minced fresh flat-leaf (Italian) parsley

¼ teaspoon red pepper flakes

1 lb (500 g) ripe plum (Roma) tomatoes, chopped

20 Kalamata olives or other brine-cured Mediterranean-style olives, pitted and coarsely chopped

4 anchovy fillets in olive oil, drained and minced

1½ tablespoons capers, rinsed and coarsely chopped

salt to taste

1 lb (500 g) dried penne

Theories abound about why this zesty tomato sauce is named for *puttane,* women in the world's oldest profession. Some surmise that it's because the sauce is so quickly made that these hard-working ladies of the evening could prepare it between clients.

SERVES 4–6

❁ In a large sauté pan over medium heat, warm the olive oil. Add the garlic, parsley, and red pepper flakes and sauté for 1 minute to release the garlic's fragrance. Add the tomatoes, raise the heat to medium-high, and simmer briskly, stirring often, until they break down and form a sauce, about 15 minutes. Reduce the heat to low. Stir in the olives, anchovies, and capers; season with salt. Remove from the heat.

❁ Bring a large pot three-fourths full of salted water to a boil over high heat. Add the pasta, stir well, and cook until al dente (firm but tender to the bite), about 12 minutes or according to the package directions. While the pasta is cooking, reheat the sauce gently over low heat.

❁ Drain the pasta and return to the warm pot. Add the sauce and toss. Divide among warmed dishes and serve at once.

NUTRITIONAL ANALYSIS PER SERVING: Calories 524 (Kilojoules 2,201); Protein 13 g; Carbohydrates 76 g; Total Fat 18 g; Saturated Fat 2 g; Cholesterol 2 mg; Sodium 917 mg; Dietary Fiber 3 g

COOKING TIP: Although penne, with its distinctive quill shape, is a favorite partner for puttanesca sauce, spaghetti or linguine can be used as well.

Bucatini with Anchovy Sauce

PREP TIME: 15 MINUTES

COOKING TIME: 12 MINUTES

INGREDIENTS

1 lb (500 g) dried bucatini, perciatelli, or spaghetti

¼ cup (2 fl oz/60 ml) olive oil

4 large cloves garlic, minced

3 tablespoons minced fresh flat-leaf (Italian) parsley

8 anchovy fillets in olive oil, drained and chopped

salt and ground pepper to taste

COOKING TIP: For a milder flavor, substitute 4 drained canned sardines for the anchovies. Carefully remove the bones and skin before incorporating them into the sauce.

For anchovy lovers, this sauce provides uncomplicated pleasure. The secret to success is not to cook the anchovies, but to let them dissolve in the residual heat of the pan.

SERVES 4–6

❀ Bring a large pot three-fourths full of salted water to a boil over high heat. Add the pasta, stir well, and cook until al dente (tender but firm to the bite), about 12 minutes or according to the package directions.

❀ While the pasta is cooking, in a large sauté pan over medium heat, warm the olive oil. Add the garlic and 2 tablespoons of the parsley and sauté for 1 minute to release the garlic's fragrance. Remove from the heat and add the anchovies. With the back of a wooden spoon, mash the anchovies until they dissolve into the oil. Season with salt and pepper. Keep warm.

❀ Using tongs, transfer the pasta, still dripping wet, to the sauté pan. (Alternatively, drain the pasta, leaving it dripping wet. Return to the warm pot and add the sauce.) Toss the pasta well with the sauce. Divide among warmed dishes. Top with the remaining 1 tablespoon parsley, dividing it evenly. Serve at once.

NUTRITIONAL ANALYSIS PER SERVING: Calories 451 (Kilojoules 1,894); Protein 14 g; Carbohydrates 69 g; Total Fat 13 g; Saturated Fat 2 g; Cholesterol 4 mg; Sodium 553 mg; Dietary Fiber 2 g

Baked Mostaccioli with Sausage and Eggplant

PREP TIME: 30 MINUTES, PLUS
2 HOURS FOR DRAINING

COOKING TIME: 45 MINUTES

INGREDIENTS

1 eggplant (aubergine), about 1 lb
(500 g)

1½ teaspoons salt, plus salt to taste

3 tablespoons olive oil

2 cloves garlic, minced

1 can (14½ oz/455 g) whole plum
(Roma) tomatoes with juice,
passed through a food mill or
puréed in a food processor

1½ teaspoons minced fresh oregano

¾ lb (375 g) hot Italian sausage,
loose or casings removed

1 lb (500 g) dried mostaccioli or
penne

½ lb (250 g) whole-milk ricotta
cheese, seasoned to taste with
salt and pepper

¼ cup (1 oz/30 g) grated Parmesan
cheese

This hearty baked pasta makes a satisfying meal with a salad of romaine (cos) lettuce and anchovies to start.

SERVES 6

✽ Trim the eggplant. Cut crosswise into rounds ¾ inch (2 cm) thick. Arrange on a rack. Sprinkle the tops with the 1½ teaspoons salt. Let stand for 2 hours. The rounds will exude moisture. Pat dry with paper towels.

✽ Preheat a broiler (griller). Oil a baking sheet. Arrange the eggplant rounds on the prepared sheet. Brush with 1 tablespoon of the olive oil. Broil (grill) about 8 inches (20 cm) from the heat until browned on the top, 4–5 minutes. Turn the rounds and brush the second side with another 1 tablespoon of the oil. Broil until browned, about 4 minutes. Let cool. Cut the rounds in half.

✽ Preheat an oven to 400°F (200°C).

✽ In a sauté pan over medium heat, warm the remaining 1 tablespoon oil. Add the garlic and sauté for 1 minute to release its fragrance. Add the tomatoes and oregano and bring to a simmer. Cook, uncovered, for about 5 minutes to blend the flavors. Add the sausage to the pan, breaking it up into bits with a fork. Continue to simmer over medium heat until the sauce is thick, about 5 minutes. Taste and adjust the seasonings.

✽ Bring a large pot three-fourths full of salted water to a boil over high heat. Add the pasta, stir well, and cook until half done, about 6 minutes. Drain and return to the warm pot. Add the sauce and toss.

✽ In an oval 9-by-14-inch (23-by-35-cm) baking dish, make a layer with one-third of the pasta. Top with half of the eggplant. Dot with half of the ricotta cheese. Repeat the layers, using half of the remaining pasta and all of the remaining eggplant and ricotta. Top with the remaining pasta and sprinkle the Parmesan evenly over the top. Cover tightly with aluminum foil.

✽ Bake until hot throughout, about 20 minutes. Remove from the oven, remove the foil, and serve at once.

NUTRITIONAL ANALYSIS PER SERVING: Calories 663 (Kilojoules 2,785); Protein 25 g; Carbohydrates 66 g; Total Fat 33 g; Saturated Fat 12 g; Cholesterol 66 mg; Sodium 1,083 mg; Dietary Fiber 3 g

"Straw and Hay" Fettuccine

PREP TIME: 45 MINUTES, PLUS
1½ HOURS IF MAKING
FRESH PASTA

COOKING TIME: 10 MINUTES

INGREDIENTS

½ oz (15 g) dried porcini mushrooms

1 cup (8 fl oz/250 ml) warm water

2 tablespoons olive oil

1 lb (500 g) skinless, boneless chicken breast, cut into bite-sized pieces

salt and ground pepper to taste

1 cup (8 fl oz/250 ml) heavy (double) cream

½ cup (4 fl oz/125 ml) chicken broth

2 cloves garlic, minced

1 teaspoon minced fresh marjoram

½ lb (250 g) fresh spinach fettuccine, homemade (page 13) or store-bought

½ lb (250 g) fresh egg fettuccine, homemade (page 13) or store-bought

2 oz (60 g) prosciutto, minced

1 cup (4 oz/120 g) grated Parmesan cheese

Ever poetic, Italians pair egg and spinach pasta and call the combination *paglia e fieno*—"straw and hay." Here, the noodles are sauced with chicken, powerfully woodsy porcini mushrooms, and herb-infused cream.

SERVES 4–6

❀ In a small bowl, combine the porcini and warm water and let stand for 30 minutes to soften the mushrooms. Remove the mushrooms and chop finely. Line a fine-mesh sieve with a double thickness of cheesecloth (muslin) and pour the soaking liquid through it into a bowl or pitcher. Set the mushrooms and liquid aside separately.

❀ Bring a large pot three-fourths full of salted water to a boil over high heat. While the water is heating, place a large sauté pan over medium-high heat. When the pan is hot, add the olive oil. When the olive oil is very hot, add the chicken and season with salt and pepper. Sauté just until the chicken is no longer pink, about 3 minutes; do not cook through at this point, as the chicken will cook more when you reheat it. Transfer to a plate.

❀ Add the cream, chicken broth, mushrooms and soaking liquid, garlic, and marjoram to the sauté pan. Simmer, uncovered, over medium-high heat until reduced to a consistency that will coat the noodles nicely, 1–2 minutes. When the sauce achieves the desired thickness, reduce the heat to low.

❀ Add all the pasta to the boiling water, stir well, and cook until al dente (tender but firm to the bite), about 2 minutes. While the pasta is cooking, return the chicken to the sauté pan and add the prosciutto. Reheat gently over low heat.

❀ Drain the pasta, reserving about 1 cup (8 fl oz/250 ml) of the cooking water, and return the pasta to the warm pot. Add the sauce and toss well. Add some of the reserved cooking water if needed to thin the sauce. If the sauce is too thin, cook the pasta briefly over high heat until it absorbs the sauce. Divide among warmed dishes. Top with ¼ cup (1 oz/30 g) Parmesan cheese, dividing it evenly. Serve at once. Pass the remaining ¾ cup (3 oz/90 g) Parmesan at the table.

NUTRITIONAL ANALYSIS PER SERVING: Calories 713 (Kilojoules 2,995); Protein 44 g; Carbohydrates 54 g; Total Fat 35 g; Saturated Fat 17 g; Cholesterol 235 mg; Sodium 1,184 mg; Dietary Fiber 3 g

Bucatini all'Amatriciana

PREP TIME: 25 MINUTES

COOKING TIME: 45 MINUTES

INGREDIENTS

2 tablespoons olive oil

⅓ lb (155 g) pancetta, diced

1 yellow onion, thinly sliced

1½ lb (750 g) ripe plum (Roma) tomatoes, peeled, seeded, and diced, or 2 cups (12 oz/375 g) chopped canned plum (Roma) tomatoes

¼ teaspoon red pepper flakes

salt to taste

1 lb (500 g) dried bucatini, perciatelli, or spaghetti

½ cup (2 oz/60 g) grated pecorino cheese

Often served in Rome's trattorias, this dish takes its name from Amatrice, a town northeast of the capital. The classic preparation calls for making a sauce of tomatoes, onion, and pancetta, and then pairing it with bucatini, a thick spaghetti-like noodle with a hole through the middle. Perciatelli is a very similar but slightly thinner noodle.

SERVES 4–6

✿ In a large sauté pan over medium heat, warm the olive oil and pancetta, stirring occasionally, until the pancetta renders some of its fat, about 3 minutes. Add the onion and sauté until softened, about 8 minutes. Add the tomatoes and red pepper flakes. Bring to a simmer, adjust the heat to maintain a simmer, and cook uncovered, stirring occasionally, for 20 minutes, adding a little water if the sauce becomes too thick. Season with salt. Remove from the heat.

✿ Bring a large pot three-fourths full of salted water to a boil over high heat. Add the pasta, stir well, and cook until al dente (tender but firm to the bite), about 12 minutes or according to the package directions. While the pasta is cooking, reheat the sauce gently over low heat.

✿ Drain the pasta and return to the warm pot. Add the sauce and ¼ cup (1 oz/30 g) of the pecorino cheese. Toss well. Divide among warmed dishes. Top with the remaining ¼ cup (1 oz/30 g) cheese, dividing it evenly. Serve at once.

NUTRITIONAL ANALYSIS PER SERVING: Calories 578 (Kilojoules 2,428); Protein 20 g; Carbohydrates 77 g; Total Fat 21 g; Saturated Fat 7 g; Cholesterol 29 mg; Sodium 843 mg; Dietary Fiber 4 g

Pappardelle with Asparagus

PREP TIME: 20 MINUTES,
    PLUS 1 HOUR IF MAKING
    FRESH PASTA

COOKING TIME: 10 MINUTES

INGREDIENTS

1½ lb (750 g) tender asparagus tips

4 tablespoons (2 oz/60 g) unsalted butter

¼ cup (1½ oz/45 g) minced shallots

2 oz (60 g) prosciutto, minced

salt and ground pepper to taste

1 lb (500 g) fresh pappardelle, homemade (page 13) or store-bought

½ cup (2 oz/60 g) grated Parmesan cheese

2 tablespoons minced fresh flat-leaf (Italian) parsley

PREP TIP: Some markets sell asparagus already trimmed down to the tender tips. If buying untrimmed asparagus, you will need to purchase about double the weight indicated in this recipe. Use 2–5 inches (5–13 cm) of the tips and reserve the stalks for another use.

The rich mixture of butter, cheese, and fresh asparagus is a perfect complement to freshly made ribbons of egg pasta. If you are not making pasta at home, purchase fresh pasta sheets and cut into ribbons ¾ inch (2 cm) wide.

SERVES 4–6

❀ Bring a large pot three-fourths full of salted water to a boil over high heat. Add the asparagus tips and cook until tender, about 5 minutes; the timing will depend upon the thickness of the spears. Drain well, then slice on the diagonal.

❀ In a large sauté pan over medium heat, melt 2 tablespoons of the butter. Add the shallots and sauté until softened, about 2 minutes. Add the prosciutto and asparagus, season well with salt and pepper, and stir to coat with the seasonings. Remove from the heat and keep warm.

❀ Again bring a large pot three-fourths full of salted water to a boil over high heat. Add the pasta, stir well, and cook until al dente (tender but firm to the bite), about 2 minutes.

❀ Drain the pasta, reserving about ½ cup (4 fl oz/125 ml) of the cooking water. Return the pasta to the warm pot. Add the remaining 2 tablespoons butter and the cheese, parsley, and asparagus mixture. Toss well. Add a little of the reserved cooking water if the noodles seem dry. Divide among warmed dishes and serve at once.

NUTRITIONAL ANALYSIS PER SERVING: Calories 485 (Kilojoules 2,037); Protein 23 g; Carbohydrates 60 g; Total Fat 18 g; Saturated Fat 9 g; Cholesterol 169 mg; Sodium 785 mg; Dietary Fiber 3 g

Cheese Ravioli with Tomato Sauce

PREP TIME: 1 HOUR, PLUS
  1 HOUR FOR MAKING
  SAUCE AND PASTA

COOKING TIME: 2 MINUTES

INGREDIENTS

FOR THE FILLING

¾ lb (375 g) whole-milk ricotta
  cheese

½ cup (2 oz/60 g) grated Parmesan
  cheese

I egg

¼ teaspoon ground nutmeg

salt and ground pepper to taste

semolina flour for dusting

Fresh Egg Pasta (page 13)

Tomato sauce from Spaghetti and
  Meatballs (page 78)

I cup (4 oz/125 g) grated Parmesan
  cheese

PREP TIP: The boiled ravioli can be
served with just butter and cheese,
instead of the tomato sauce.

Delicate homemade ravioli surpass anything you can buy. Recruit
a helper, if possible, to make the work go faster. The tomato
sauce can be made a day ahead and reheated before tossing
with the boiled ravioli.

SERVES 4–6

❋ To make the filling, in a bowl, combine the ricotta and Parmesan
cheeses, egg, and nutmeg. Mix well with a fork. Season with salt and
pepper. Cover and refrigerate until needed.

❋ Heavily dust several baking sheets with semolina flour. Following the
directions on page 12, roll out the pasta dough to make the thinnest possible sheets. Working with 1 pasta sheet at a time, place on a work surface dusted with semolina flour with the longer side of the pasta facing
you. Measure the width of the pasta sheet (the shorter dimension) and
divide by two to give you the size of the finished ravioli. (For example,
a pasta sheet 6 inches/15 cm wide will make ravioli 3 inches/7.5 cm
square.) To guide you in placing the filling, notch the long edge of the
pasta sheet with a pastry wheel to mark the ravioli size. Put about 1½ teaspoons filling in the center of the ravioli on the bottom half of the pasta
sheet. Moisten the dough edges lightly with water. Fold over the top half
of the sheet, matching the edges. Press firmly between and around the
ravioli to seal well.

❋ Using a fluted pastry wheel, cut between the ravioli. Transfer to the
prepared baking sheets. Repeat with the remaining pasta sheets. You
should have at least 4 dozen ravioli. Let dry for 30 minutes at room
temperature.

❋ Bring a large pot three-fourths full of salted water to a boil over high
heat. Meanwhile, reheat the tomato sauce gently over low heat; keep warm.

❋ Add the ravioli to the boiling water, stir gently, and then cook at a
gentle boil until al dente (tender but firm to the bite), about 1½ minutes.
Using a large sieve, transfer the ravioli to a warmed serving bowl. Add
the sauce and toss gently. Divide among warmed bowls. Top each portion with a little of the Parmesan cheese and serve at once. Pass the
remaining Parmesan at the table.

NUTRITIONAL ANALYSIS PER SERVING: Calories 712 (Kilojoules 2,990); Protein 34 g;
Carbohydrates 67 g; Total Fat 33 g; Saturated Fat 14 g; Cholesterol 228 mg; Sodium 1,233 mg;
Dietary Fiber 3 g

Penne alla Norma

PREP TIME: 30 MINUTES, PLUS
1 HOUR FOR DRAINING

COOKING TIME: 1¼ HOURS

INGREDIENTS

1 eggplant (aubergine), about 1 lb (500 g), cut into ¾-inch (2-cm) cubes

2 teaspoons salt, plus salt to taste

4 tablespoons (2 fl oz/60 ml) olive oil

3 cloves garlic, minced

pinch of red pepper flakes

1 lb (500 g) ripe plum (Roma) tomatoes, diced

12 fresh basil leaves, torn into small pieces

1 lb (500 g) dried penne

½ cup (2 oz/60 g) grated pecorino cheese

Some food scholars contend that this pasta is named for the most famous opera of Vincenzo Bellini, a Sicilian composer. True or not, eggplant and tomato are popular partners for pasta in Sicily—indeed, throughout southern Italy.

SERVES 4–6

❋ In a bowl, toss the eggplant cubes with the 2 teaspoons salt. Transfer to a sieve or colander and let stand for 1 hour. The cubes will exude moisture. Pat dry with paper towels.

❋ In a large sauté pan over medium heat, warm 2 tablespoons of the olive oil. Add the garlic and red pepper flakes and sauté for 1 minute to release the garlic's fragrance. Add the tomatoes, raise the heat to medium-high, and simmer briskly, stirring often, until the tomatoes break down and form a sauce, about 15 minutes. Add a little water if the sauce becomes too thick. Season with salt, then stir in the basil. Remove from the heat.

❋ In a large nonstick sauté pan over medium-high heat, warm 1 tablespoon of the remaining olive oil. Add half of the eggplant and sauté until well browned, about 10 minutes. Transfer to the pan holding the tomato sauce. Repeat with the remaining 1 tablespoon oil and the remaining eggplant.

❋ Bring the eggplant and sauce to a simmer over medium heat, adding a little water if needed to thin the sauce. Cover and adjust the heat to maintain a gentle simmer. Cook until the eggplant is soft but not mushy, 15–20 minutes. Remove from the heat.

❋ Bring a large pot three-fourths full of salted water to a boil over high heat. Add the pasta, stir well, and cook until al dente (tender but firm to the bite), about 12 minutes or according to the package directions. While the pasta is cooking, reheat the sauce gently over low heat. Drain the pasta, reserving about 1 cup (8 fl oz/250 ml) of the cooking water. Return the pasta to the warm pot. Add the sauce and toss. Add ¼ cup (1 oz/30 g) of the pecorino cheese and toss again, adding some of the reserved water if needed to thin the sauce. Divide among warmed dishes. Top with the remaining ¼ cup (1 oz/30 g) pecorino cheese, dividing it evenly. Serve at once.

NUTRITIONAL ANALYSIS PER SERVING: Calories 524 (Kilojoules 2,201); Protein 16 g; Carbohydrates 78 g; Total Fat 16 g; Saturated Fat 4 g; Cholesterol 11 mg; Sodium 829 mg; Dietary Fiber 5 g

Spinach Lasagne with Meat Sauce

PREP TIME: 1 HOUR, PLUS
  1¼ HOURS FOR MAKING
  PASTA

COOKING TIME: 1 HOUR, PLUS
  4½ HOURS FOR MAKING
  SAUCE

INGREDIENTS

¼ cup (2 oz/60 g) unsalted butter

¼ cup (1½ oz/45 g) unbleached all-
  purpose (plain) flour

3 cups (24 fl oz/750 ml) milk

4 fresh thyme sprigs

1 bay leaf

freshly grated nutmeg to taste

salt and ground pepper to taste

Fresh Spinach Pasta *(page 13)*

ice water

1 tablespoon olive oil

Bolognese sauce *(page 96)* or 3 cups
  (24 fl oz/750 ml) store-bought
  meat sauce

1 cup (4 oz/125 g) grated Parmesan
  cheese

Open a fine red wine for this elegant lasagne—a dozen layers of thin spinach noodles, rich meat sauce, and creamy béchamel.

SERVES 6–8

❀ Melt the butter in a saucepan over medium heat. Add the flour and whisk to blend. Cook, whisking constantly, for 1 minute. Add the milk and bring to a simmer, whisking. Add the thyme and bay leaf, and season with nutmeg, salt, and pepper. Reduce the heat to low and cook gently, whisking often, for about 30 minutes. Press the béchamel through a coarse-mesh sieve into a bowl; let cool.

❀ Preheat an oven to 400°F (200°C). Following the directions on page 12, roll the pasta dough into thin sheets. Fill a large bowl three-fourths full of ice water and add the olive oil. Bring a large pot three-fourths full of salted water to a boil. Cook the pasta sheets, 2 sheets at a time, for 10 seconds only. Transfer to the ice water and unfurl the sheets in the water, then lay flat on a kitchen towel and pat dry.

❀ Pour a thin layer of the béchamel sauce into a 9-by-13-inch (23-by-33-cm) baking dish. Top with a layer of pasta, cutting the sheets to fit. Spread 3 tablespoons béchamel sauce thinly and evenly over the pasta, then spread about ⅓ cup (3 fl oz/80 ml) of the Bolognese sauce thinly over the béchamel. Sprinkle with a generous tablespoon of the Parmesan cheese. Continue making layers of pasta, béchamel, Bolognese sauce, and Parmesan until you use up all the sauces, reserving ⅓ cup (3 fl oz/80 ml) béchamel for the top. You should have enough to make 10–12 layers of pasta and sauce. Finish with a layer of pasta topped with the reserved béchamel sauce and 2 tablespoons Parmesan.

❀ Bake, uncovered, until puffed and bubbling, 25–30 minutes. If desired, place under a preheated broiler (griller) briefly to brown the surface. Let cool for 15 minutes, then cut into squares to serve.

NUTRITIONAL ANALYSIS PER SERVING: Calories 765 (Kilojoules 3,213); Protein 32 g; Carbohydrates 68 g; Total Fat 40 g; Saturated Fat 18 g; Cholesterol 161 mg; Sodium 619 mg; Dietary Fiber 4 g

Spaghettini with Tomatoes and Arugula

PREP TIME: 15 MINUTES

COOKING TIME: 15 MINUTES

INGREDIENTS

¼ cup (2 fl oz/60 ml) olive oil

4 cloves garlic, minced

⅛ teaspoon red pepper flakes

1 lb (500 g) ripe plum (Roma) tomatoes, diced

salt to taste

1 lb (500 g) dried spaghettini

⅓ lb (5 oz/155 g) arugula, thick stems removed and large leaves coarsely chopped

PREP TIP: Seek out young, tender arugula; older arugula leaves can have a peppery bite.

This summery sauce can be made in the time it takes to boil the pasta. Its lightness makes it appropriate for thin strands like spaghettini. If desired, serve with grated Parmesan cheese.

SERVES 4–6

❀ In a large sauté pan over medium heat, warm the olive oil. Add the garlic and red pepper flakes and sauté for 1 minute to release the garlic's fragrance. Add the tomatoes, season generously with salt, and cook gently until the tomatoes begin to release some of their liquid but still retain their shape, 3–4 minutes. Remove from the heat.

❀ Bring a large pot three-fourths full of salted water to a boil over high heat. Add the pasta, stir well, and cook until al dente (tender but firm to the bite), about 10 minutes or according to the package directions. While the pasta is cooking, reheat the sauce gently over low heat.

❀ Drain the pasta and return to the warm pot. Add the sauce and arugula and toss. The arugula will wilt from the heat of the pasta. Divide among warmed dishes and serve at once.

NUTRITIONAL ANALYSIS PER SERVING: Calories 458 (Kilojoules 1,924); Protein 13 g; Carbohydrates 73 g; Total Fat 13 g; Saturated Fat 2 g; Cholesterol 0 mg; Sodium 336 mg; Dietary Fiber 4 g

Fettuccine with Artichokes, Prosciutto, and Cream

PREP TIME: 30 MINUTES, PLUS
1 HOUR IF MAKING FRESH
PASTA

COOKING TIME: 25 MINUTES

INGREDIENTS

juice of 1 lemon

16 small artichokes, about 2 oz
(60 g) each

2 tablespoons olive oil

½ yellow onion, chopped

1 cup (8 fl oz/250 ml) chicken broth

salt and ground pepper to taste

1 cup (8 fl oz/250 ml) heavy (double)
cream

2 oz (60 g) prosciutto, minced

2 tablespoons minced fresh flat-leaf
(Italian) parsley

1 lb (500 g) fresh fettuccine, homemade (page 13) or store-bought

PREP TIP: Small, immature artichokes
have not yet developed their fibrous
chokes. If you can find only larger
artichokes, buy fewer and trim
them following the instructions for
Artichokes, Roman Style (page 25),
then slice them as directed in
this recipe.

Serve this rich pasta with light accompaniments before and after.

SERVES 4–6

❋ Fill a bowl three-fourths full of water and add the lemon juice.
Working with 1 artichoke at a time and starting at the base, break off
about 3 or 4 rows of the tough outer leaves, snapping them downward,
until you reach the pale yellow-green inner leaves. Cut off about ⅓ inch
(9 mm) from the top of the artichoke. Using a small, sharp knife, cut
off the stem flush with the bottom of the artichoke and then trim away
any tough green parts from the base. Drop the trimmed artichoke into
the lemon water to prevent browning, and put an inverted plate in the
bowl to keep it submerged. Repeat with the remaining artichokes.

❋ In a large sauté pan over medium heat, warm the olive oil. Add the
onion and sauté until softened, about 5 minutes.

❋ While the onion is sautéing, halve the artichokes and slice thinly
lengthwise. Add to the pan along with ½ cup (4 fl oz/125 ml) of the
chicken broth. Season with salt and pepper if needed. Bring to a simmer over medium-high heat, cover, and adjust the heat to maintain a
gentle simmer. Cook until the artichokes are tender, about 15 minutes.
Uncover and add the remaining ½ cup (4 fl oz/125 ml) broth and the
cream. Return to a simmer and simmer, uncovered, until the mixture
thickens slightly. Stir in the prosciutto and parsley. Taste and adjust
the seasonings. Remove from the heat.

❋ Bring a large pot three-fourths full of salted water to a boil over high
heat. Meanwhile, reheat the sauce gently over low heat, then add the
pasta to the boiling water. Stir well and cook until al dente (tender but
firm to the bite), about 2 minutes. Drain the pasta, reserving about 1 cup
(8 fl oz/250 ml) of the cooking water. Return the pasta to the warm pot.
Add the sauce and toss, adding some of the reserved water if needed to
thin the sauce. Divide among warmed dishes and serve at once.

NUTRITIONAL ANALYSIS PER SERVING: Calories 601 (Kilojoules 2,524); Protein 19 g;
Carbohydrates 68 g; Total Fat 29 g; Saturated Fat 13 g; Cholesterol 202 mg; Sodium 962 mg;
Dietary Fiber 8 g

Spaghetti with Seafood

PREP TIME: 45 MINUTES

COOKING TIME: 30 MINUTES

INGREDIENTS

1 lb (500 g) squid

1 lb (500 g) mussels

4 tablespoons (2 fl oz/60 ml) olive oil

4 cloves garlic, minced

pinch of red pepper flakes

1 can (14½ oz/455 g) whole plum (Roma) tomatoes with juice, passed through a food mill or puréed in a food processor

salt to taste

12 fresh basil leaves, torn into small pieces

1 lb (500 g) dried spaghetti

½ cup (⅔ oz/20 g) minced fresh flat-leaf (Italian) parsley

½ cup (4 fl oz/125 ml) dry white wine

½ lb (250 g) large shrimp (prawns), peeled, halved lengthwise, and deveined

The ancient Sicilian city of Siracusa is famous for its seafood. This mixed-seafood pasta is typical of the region.

SERVES 4–6

✺ To clean each squid, grasp the head and pull it and the attached innards free of the body. Cut off and discard the part below the tentacles that contains the eyes, then squeeze out and discard the beak at the base of the tentacles. Cut the tentacles in half lengthwise if large, and set aside. Rinse the body cavity with running water, removing and discarding the quill-like cartilage lodged inside. Rub off the brownish skin from the body, then cut the body crosswise into rings ¼ inch (6 mm) wide. Discard any mussels that do not stay closed when gently pressed, then scrub well under cold running water and pull off and discard the beards. Set the squid and mussels aside.

✺ In a sauté pan over medium heat, warm 2 tablespoons of the olive oil. Add half of the garlic and the red pepper flakes and sauté for 1 minute to release the garlic's fragrance. Add the tomatoes and season with salt. Simmer gently, stirring occasionally, until the sauce is thick and tasty, about 15 minutes. Stir in the basil. Keep warm over low heat.

✺ Bring a large pot three-fourths full of salted water to a boil over high heat. Add the pasta, stir well, and cook until al dente (tender but firm to the bite), about 12 minutes or according to the package directions. When the spaghetti is 8 minutes short of being ready, heat the remaining 2 tablespoons olive oil in a large sauté pan over medium-high heat. Add the remaining garlic and ¼ cup (⅓ oz/10 g) of the parsley. Sauté briefly to release the garlic's fragrance. Add the white wine and simmer briskly for about 1 minute, then add the mussels. Cover and cook until the mussels open, about 2 minutes, then add the squid and shrimp. Stir, cover, and cook, stirring once or twice, for 1–2 minutes. Remove from the heat. Discard any mussels that did not open.

✺ Drain the pasta and return to the warm pot. Add the tomato sauce and toss. Add the seafood and their juices and toss gently. Divide among warmed dishes. Top with the remaining ¼ cup (⅓ oz/10 g) parsley, dividing it evenly. Serve at once.

NUTRITIONAL ANALYSIS PER SERVING: Calories 636 (Kilojoules 2,671); Protein 42 g; Carbohydrates 76 g; Total Fat 15 g; Saturated Fat 2 g; Cholesterol 284 mg; Sodium 669 mg; Dietary Fiber 3 g

Linguine with Clams

PREP TIME: 20 MINUTES

COOKING TIME: 30 MINUTES

INGREDIENTS

4 dozen small clams, about 2 lb
   (1 kg) (see note)

½ cup (4 fl oz/125 ml) dry white wine

½ cup (4 fl oz/125 ml) water

¼ cup (2 fl oz/60 ml) olive oil

1 small yellow onion, minced

4 cloves garlic, minced

¼ cup (⅓ oz/10 g) minced fresh
   flat-leaf (Italian) parsley

¼ teaspoon red pepper flakes

1 lb (500 g) dried linguine

salt to taste

Parsley, garlic, and red pepper flakes give this clam sauce its fresh, lively character. Varieties of small clams appropriate for this recipe include littleneck, cherrystone, butter, and Manila.

SERVES 4–6

❋ Discard any clams that do not stay closed when gently pressed, then scrub the clams well under cold running water. In a large pot, combine the wine and water. Bring to a simmer, add the clams, cover, and cook, shaking the pot once or twice to redistribute the clams, just until the clams open, about 3 minutes. Using a slotted spoon, transfer the clams to a bowl, discarding any that did not open. Line a fine-mesh sieve with a triple thickness of cheesecloth (muslin) and pour the cooking liquid through it into a pitcher or bowl. Set the clams and strained liquid aside.

❋ In a large sauté pan over medium heat, warm the olive oil. Add the onion and sauté until soft, about 10 minutes. Add the garlic, parsley, and red pepper flakes and sauté for 1 minute to release the garlic's fragrance. Remove from the heat.

❋ Bring a large pot three-fourths full of salted water to a boil over high heat. Add the pasta, stir well, and cook until al dente (tender but firm to the bite), about 10 minutes or according to the package directions. Just before the pasta is done, add the strained clam liquid to the sauté pan and reheat over medium heat. Season with salt. Reduce the heat to low, add the clams, and reheat gently.

❋ Drain the pasta and return to the warm pot. Add the sauce and toss well. Divide among warmed dishes and serve at once.

NUTRITIONAL ANALYSIS PER SERVING: Calories 482 (Kilojoules 2,024); Protein 16 g; Carbohydrates 72 g; Total Fat 13 g; Saturated Fat 2 g; Cholesterol 9 mg; Sodium 335 mg; Dietary Fiber 3 g

Mushroom Lasagne

PREP TIME: 1 HOUR, PLUS
    1 HOUR FOR MAKING PASTA

COOKING TIME: 2 HOURS

INGREDIENTS

1 oz (30 g) dried porcini mushrooms

1½ cups (12 fl oz/375 ml) warm water

¼ cup (2 oz/60 g) unsalted butter

¼ cup (1½ oz/45 g) unbleached all-
    purpose (plain) flour

2½ cups (20 fl oz/625 ml) milk

4 fresh thyme sprigs

1 bay leaf

freshly grated nutmeg to taste

salt and ground pepper to taste

5 tablespoons (3 fl oz/80 ml) olive oil

1 yellow onion, chopped

2 cloves garlic, minced

2 tablespoons minced fresh flat-leaf
    (Italian) parsley

1 tablespoon minced fresh sage

1 can (14½ oz/455 g) whole plum
    (Roma) tomatoes, passed through
    a food mill or puréed in a food
    processor

2 lb (1 kg) fresh mushrooms, brushed
    clean, halved if large, and thinly
    sliced

1½ lb (750 g) Fresh Egg Pasta
    (page 13)

ice water

1 cup (4 oz/125 g) grated Parmesan
    cheese

SERVES 6–8

❈ In a bowl, combine the porcini and warm water; let stand for 30 minutes. Using a slotted spoon, lift out the porcini and finely chop. Strain the soaking liquid through a fine-mesh sieve lined with cheese-cloth (muslin) into a bowl. Melt the butter in a saucepan over medium heat. Add the flour and cook, whisking constantly, for 1 minute. Add the milk and ½ cup (4 fl oz/125 ml) of the soaking liquid. Bring to a simmer, whisking. Add the herbs and season with nutmeg, salt, and pepper. Cook gently over low heat, whisking often, for about 30 minutes. Press through a coarse-mesh sieve into a bowl and set aside.

❈ In a sauté pan over medium heat, warm 2 tablespoons of the olive oil. Add the onion and sauté until soft. Add the garlic and sauté for 1 minute. Add the parsley, sage, tomatoes, and season with salt and pepper. Bring to a simmer and cook until thick, about 10 minutes. In another sauté pan, heat 2 tablespoons of the remaining olive oil over high heat. Add the fresh mushrooms, season with salt and pepper, and sauté until the liquid they render evaporates, about 10 minutes. Add the tomato sauce, porcini, and enough of the soaking liquid to thin the sauce. Cover and simmer for 10 minutes.

❈ Preheat an oven to 400°F (200°C). Following the directions on page 12, roll out the pasta dough into thin sheets. Fill a large bowl three-fourths full with ice water and add the remaining 1 tablespoon olive oil. Bring a large pot three-fourths full of salted water to a boil. Cook the pasta, 2 sheets at a time, for 10 seconds only. Transfer to the ice water and unfurl the sheets in the water, then lay flat on a kitchen towel and pat dry.

❈ Pour a thin layer of the cream sauce into a 9-by-13-inch (23-by-33-cm) baking dish. Top with a layer of pasta, cutting the sheets to fit. Spread 3 tablespoons cream sauce over the pasta, then spread on a scant ½ cup (4 fl oz/ 125 ml) tomato-mushroom sauce. Sprinkle with a generous tablespoon of the Parmesan. Continue making layers, reserving ⅓ cup (3 fl oz/80 ml) cream sauce for the top. You should have enough to make 10–12 layers of pasta and sauce. Finish with a layer of pasta topped with the cream sauce and 2 tablespoons Parmesan. Bake, uncovered, until puffed and bubbling, 25–30 minutes. Let cool for 15 minutes, then serve.

NUTRITIONAL ANALYSIS PER SERVING: Calories 671 (Kilojoules 2,818); Protein 26 g; Carbohydrates 79 g; Total Fat 28 g; Saturated Fat 11 g; Cholesterol 178 mg; Sodium 780 mg; Dietary Fiber 6 g

Spaghetti and Meatballs

PREP TIME: 1 HOUR

COOKING TIME: 30 MINUTES

INGREDIENTS

FOR THE MEATBALLS

½ lb (250 g) ground (minced) veal

½ lb (250 g) ground (minced) pork

2 eggs, lightly beaten

½ small yellow onion, minced

½ cup (2 oz/60 g) fine dried bread crumbs (see glossary, page 108)

¼ cup (1 oz/30 g) grated Parmesan cheese

1 tablespoon minced fresh flat-leaf (Italian) parsley

2 teaspoons minced fresh oregano

½ teaspoon fennel seeds, preferably lightly crushed in a mortar

1½ teaspoons salt

ground pepper to taste

FOR THE TOMATO SAUCE

¼ cup (2 fl oz/60 ml) olive oil

4 cloves garlic, minced

1 tablespoon minced fresh flat-leaf (Italian) parsley

pinch of red pepper flakes (optional)

2 cans (14½ oz/455 g each) whole plum (Roma) tomatoes, finely chopped, with juice

salt to taste

1 lb (500 g) dried spaghetti

1 cup (4 oz/125 g) grated Parmesan cheese

Fresh oregano and fragrant fennel seeds make these meatballs particularly tasty. If pressed for time, substitute a large jar (26–28 fl oz/810–875 ml) of store-bought spaghetti sauce for the homemade sauce. Try to time the cooking so that the meatballs and pasta are done at the same time.

SERVES 4–6

❀ To make the meatballs, in a large bowl, combine the ground meats, eggs, onion, bread crumbs, Parmesan cheese, parsley, oregano, fennel seeds, salt, and pepper to taste. Mix gently with your hands until blended. Shape the mixture into 24 meatballs, working gently and dipping your hands in cold water to prevent sticking. Put the meatballs in a single layer on a large plate and refrigerate.

❀ To make the tomato sauce, in a large sauté pan over medium heat, warm the olive oil. Add the garlic, the parsley, and the red pepper flakes, if using. Sauté for 1 minute to release the garlic's fragrance. Add the tomatoes and simmer, uncovered, until the flavors are blended, about 15 minutes. Pass the sauce through a food mill or purée in a food processor, and then return to the pan. Season with salt. Bring to a simmer over medium heat.

❀ Add the meatballs to the sauce, cover, and adjust the heat so the sauce simmers gently. Cook for 15 minutes, turning the meatballs halfway through the cooking time.

❀ While the meatballs are cooking, bring a large pot three-fourths full of salted water to a boil over high heat. Add the pasta, stir well, and cook until al dente (tender but firm to the bite), about 12 minutes or according to the package directions. Drain and return to the warm pot. Add the meatballs and sauce and toss gently. Divide among warmed dishes. Top each portion with a little of the Parmesan cheese. Pass the remaining Parmesan cheese at the table.

NUTRITIONAL ANALYSIS PER SERVING: Calories 845 (Kilojoules 3,549); Protein 44 g; Carbohydrates 86 g; Total Fat 35 g; Saturated Fat 12 g; Cholesterol 174 mg; Sodium 1,885 mg; Dietary Fiber 4 g

Farfalle with Peas and Prosciutto

PREP TIME: 15 MINUTES

COOKING TIME: 30 MINUTES

INGREDIENTS

2 tablespoons olive oil

1 large yellow onion, halved and thinly sliced

1 package (10 oz/315 g) frozen petite peas

½ cup (4 fl oz/125 ml) water

salt and ground pepper to taste

1 lb (500 g) dried farfalle

2 oz (60 g) prosciutto, minced

2 tablespoons minced fresh flat-leaf (Italian) parsley

2 tablespoons unsalted butter

¾ cup (3 oz/90 g) grated Parmesan cheese

COOKING TIP: If you are fortunate enough to find fresh peas, you can substitute 2 cups (10 oz/315 g) shelled small, fresh peas for the frozen peas. Add them to the onion with the water as directed, cover, and simmer until done, about 5 minutes.

Make this easy pasta the centerpiece of a light spring or summer meal. Vegetarians can leave out the prosciutto, and the results will still be delicious.

SERVES 4–6

✸ In a large sauté pan over medium heat, warm the olive oil. Add the onion and sauté until it is soft and beginning to caramelize, about 15 minutes. Add the peas and water, and season with salt and pepper. Bring to a simmer and cook uncovered, stirring often, until the peas have thawed, about 5 minutes. Remove from the heat.

✸ Bring a large pot three-fourths full of salted water to a boil over high heat. Add the pasta, stir well, and cook until al dente (tender but firm to the bite), about 12 minutes or according to the package directions. While the pasta is cooking, reheat the pea mixture gently over low heat. Stir in the prosciutto and parsley.

✸ Drain the pasta and return to the warm pot. Add the butter and toss until it melts. Add the pea mixture and toss again. Divide among warmed dishes. Top each portion with a little of the Parmesan cheese. Pass the remaining Parmesan at the table.

NUTRITIONAL ANALYSIS PER SERVING: Calories 572 (Kilojoules 2,402); Protein 24 g; Carbohydrates 79 g; Total Fat 18 g; Saturated Fat 7 g; Cholesterol 33 mg; Sodium 872 mg; Dietary Fiber 6 g

Trenette with Pesto

PREP TIME: 15 MINUTES,
  PLUS 1 HOUR IF MAKING
  FRESH PASTA

COOKING TIME: 12 MINUTES

INGREDIENTS

¼ cup (1½ oz/45 g) pine nuts

1½ cups (1½ oz/45 g) fresh basil
leaves

2 cloves garlic, thinly sliced

⅓ cup (3 fl oz/80 ml) olive oil

2 tablespoons unsalted butter,
at room temperature

3 tablespoons grated pecorino
cheese

3 tablespoons grated Parmesan
cheese

salt to taste

1 lb (500 g) fresh trenette, homemade
(*page 13*) or store-bought

STORAGE TIP: If your garden yields a bumper crop of basil, you can make extra pesto and store it. To refrigerate, put the pesto in a storage container, smooth the surface, and top with a film of olive oil. Cover with plastic wrap and use within 2–3 days. To freeze, put in small freezer containers and use within 2 months, defrosting in the refrigerator before use.

Genoa claims to be the birthplace of pesto, the creamy herb sauce that derives its name from the Italian verb *pestare* (to pound). In the past, cooks made pesto in a mortar, grinding it tediously by hand with a pestle. Today, a food processor makes quick work of the task. Trenette, ribbon noodles similar to fettuccine, is the classic pasta for pesto in Genoa.

SERVES 4–6

✳ Preheat an oven to 325°F (165°C). Spread the pine nuts in a pie pan and toast until fragrant and golden, about 10 minutes. Remove from the oven and let cool.

✳ In a food processor, combine the pine nuts, basil, and garlic. Process until well chopped, stopping the processor once or twice to scrape down the sides of the work bowl. With the motor running, add the olive oil through the feed tube in a slow, steady stream. Then add the butter and process until incorporated. Transfer to a small bowl. Stir in the pecorino and Parmesan cheeses and a generous amount of salt.

✳ Bring a large pot three-fourths full of salted water to a boil over high heat. Add the pasta, stir well, and cook until al dente (tender but firm to the bite), about 2 minutes. Just before the pasta is done, thin the pesto by whisking in 4–6 tablespoons (2–3 fl oz/60–90 ml) of the hot pasta water.

✳ Transfer the thinned pesto to a warmed serving bowl. Drain the pasta and add to the bowl. Toss well. Divide among warmed dishes and serve.

NUTRITIONAL ANALYSIS PER SERVING: Calories 540 (Kilojoules 2,268); Protein 15 g; Carbohydrates 55 g; Total Fat 29 g; Saturated Fat 8 g; Cholesterol 146 mg; Sodium 497 mg; Dietary Fiber 3 g

Linguine alla Marinara

PREP TIME: 15 MINUTES

COOKING TIME: 35 MINUTES

INGREDIENTS

¼ cup (2 fl oz/60 ml) olive oil

3 cloves garlic, minced

pinch of red pepper flakes (optional)

1½ lb (750 g) ripe plum (Roma) tomatoes, diced

salt to taste

12–16 fresh basil leaves, torn into small pieces

1 lb (500 g) dried linguine

STORAGE TIP: If you are blessed with an abundance of summer tomatoes, make extra batches of this simple sauce and store in airtight freezer containers. Use within 2 months.

Why did this simple tomato-sauce preparation come to be known as *alla marinara* (sailor's style)? Perhaps because the sailor's wife could make it quickly when her seafaring husband arrived home, or perhaps because it complements seafood. You can add a handful of shrimp (prawns) to the sauce, or steam clams or mussels in it, before tossing it with pasta.

SERVES 4–6

❀ In a large sauté pan over medium heat, warm the olive oil. Add the garlic and the red pepper flakes, if using, and sauté for 1 minute to release the garlic's fragrance. Add the tomatoes and season with salt. Raise the heat to medium-high, bring to a simmer, and cook briskly, stirring often, until the tomatoes break down and form a sauce, about 15 minutes. Add a little water if the sauce becomes too thick. Pass the sauce through a food mill or purée in a food processor. Return to the pan and add the basil. Simmer gently for 5 minutes to blend the flavors, then taste and adjust the seasonings. Remove from the heat.

❀ Bring a large pot three-fourths full of salted water to a boil over high heat. Add the pasta, stir well, and cook until al dente (tender but firm to the bite), about 10 minutes or according to the package directions. While the pasta is cooking, reheat the sauce gently over low heat.

❀ Drain the pasta and return to the warm pot. Add the sauce and toss. Divide among warmed dishes and serve.

NUTRITIONAL ANALYSIS PER SERVING: Calories 464 (Kilojoules 1,949); Protein 13 g; Carbohydrates 75 g; Total Fat 13 g; Saturated Fat 2 g; Cholesterol 0 mg; Sodium 329 mg; Dietary Fiber 4 g

Orecchiette with Broccoli Rabe

PREP TIME: 15 MINUTES

COOKING TIME: 20 MINUTES

INGREDIENTS

⅓ cup (3 fl oz/80 ml) extra-virgin olive oil

8 cloves garlic, thinly sliced

¼ teaspoon red pepper flakes

ice water

1½ lb (750 g) trimmed broccoli rabe (stems thicker than a pencil removed; about 2 lb/1 kg before trimming)

1 lb (500 g) dried orecchiette

salt to taste

1 cup (4 oz/125 g) grated pecorino cheese

PREP TIP: This preparation also works well with mildly bitter kale, collard greens, or mustard greens. Remove the tough stems and ribs before using.

This straightforward preparation is enjoyed throughout Apulia, the "heel" of Italy's boot, where it is liberally drizzled with the region's superb extra-virgin olive oil. Look for broccoli rabe in specialty markets; it resembles broccoli but has thinner stems, smaller florets, and more leaves. If you can't find it, substitute broccoli florets.

SERVES 4–6

❀ In a large sauté pan over medium heat, warm the olive oil. Add the garlic and red pepper flakes and sauté until the garlic colors lightly, 1–2 minutes. Set aside.

❀ Have ready a bowl of ice water. Bring a large pot three-fourths full of salted water to a boil over high heat. Add the broccoli rabe and cook until just tender, 2–4 minutes. Using tongs, lift out and transfer to the ice water to stop the cooking. Leave the pot of water over high heat. Drain the broccoli rabe well and squeeze gently to remove any excess moisture. Chop into 2-inch (5-cm) lengths.

❀ Add the pasta to the boiling water used to cook the broccoli rabe, stir well, and cook until al dente (tender but firm to the bite), about 12 minutes or according to the package directions. While the pasta is cooking, add the broccoli rabe to the pan holding the garlic. Return to medium heat, season generously with salt, and cook, stirring occasionally, until the broccoli is hot throughout, 3–5 minutes.

❀ Drain the pasta and return to the warm pot. Add the sauce and toss. Divide among warmed dishes and serve at once. Pass the pecorino cheese at the table.

NUTRITIONAL ANALYSIS PER SERVING: Calories 586 (Kilojoules 2,461); Protein 20 g; Carbohydrates 74 g; Total Fat 23 g; Saturated Fat 7 g; Cholesterol 23 mg; Sodium 905 mg; Dietary Fiber 2 g

Spaghetti with Tuna and Sweet Peppers

PREP TIME: 25 MINUTES

COOKING TIME: 1 HOUR

INGREDIENTS

¼ cup (2 fl oz/60 ml) olive oil

2 cloves garlic, minced

⅛ teaspoon red pepper flakes

1 can (14½ oz/455 g) whole plum
   (Roma) tomatoes with juice,
   passed through a food mill or
   puréed in a food processor

¾ teaspoon fennel seeds, crushed in
   a spice grinder or mortar

salt to taste

1 red bell pepper (capsicum), halved,
   seeded, and thinly sliced lengthwise

1 yellow or green bell pepper
   (capsicum), halved, seeded, and
   thinly sliced lengthwise

¾ lb (375 g) fresh tuna fillet, cut into
   ¾-inch (2-cm) cubes

1 lb (500 g) dried spaghetti

2 tablespoons minced fresh flat-leaf
   (Italian) parsley

COOKING TIP: Although this recipe
is at its best made with fresh tuna,
drained oil-packed Italian canned tuna
can also be used. Cook the tomato-
and-pepper mixture for 30–35 minutes, until it reaches a saucelike consistency. Then add the canned tuna,
mashing it into the sauce, before
proceeding with the recipe.

Aromatic fennel seeds give this sauce its seductive flavor. Serve
with a chilled white wine or a light-bodied red.

SERVES 4–6

❀ In a large sauté pan over medium heat, warm the olive oil. Add the
garlic and red pepper flakes and sauté for 1 minute to release the garlic's
fragrance. Add the tomatoes and fennel seeds, and season with salt.
Simmer, uncovered, until thickened, about 10 minutes.

❀ Stir in the bell peppers, cover, and adjust the heat to maintain a
gentle simmer. Cook, stirring once or twice, until the peppers are soft,
about 20 minutes. Stir in the tuna, cover, and simmer until opaque
throughout, 10–15 minutes longer. Using a wooden spoon, mash the
tuna until no large pieces remain. Taste and adjust the seasonings.
Remove from the heat.

❀ Bring a large pot three-fourths full of salted water to a boil over high
heat. Add the pasta, stir well, and cook until al dente (tender but firm to
the bite), about 12 minutes or according to the package directions. Just
before the pasta is done, reheat the sauce gently over low heat.

❀ Drain the pasta, reserving about 1 cup (8 fl oz/250 ml) of the cooking
water. Return the pasta to the warm pot and add the sauce. Toss well,
adding a little of the reserved cooking water if needed to thin the sauce.
Divide among warmed dishes. Top with the parsley, dividing it evenly.
Serve at once.

NUTRITIONAL ANALYSIS PER SERVING: Calories 558 (Kilojoules 2,344); Protein 29 g;
Carbohydrates 74 g; Total Fat 16 g; Saturated Fat 3 g; Cholesterol 26 mg; Sodium 556 mg;
Dietary Fiber 3 g

Cavatappi with Sausage and Tomato

PREP TIME: 20 MINUTES

COOKING TIME: 30 MINUTES

INGREDIENTS

1 tablespoon olive oil

¾ lb (375 g) hot Italian sausage with fennel seed, loose or casings removed

1 lb (500 g) ripe plum (Roma) tomatoes, peeled, seeded, and diced

2 tablespoons minced fresh flat-leaf (Italian) parsley

½ cup (4 fl oz/125 ml) heavy (double) cream

salt and ground pepper to taste

1 lb (500 g) dried cavatappi or fusilli

1 cup (4 oz/125 g) grated Parmesan cheese

The wide grooves of cavatappi, a corkscrew-shaped pasta, trap the bits of sausage in this creamy sauce. If you can't find a sausage flavored with fennel, add ½ teaspoon fennel seeds, preferably lightly crushed in a spice grinder or mortar, at the same time that you add the sausage to the pan.

SERVES 4–6

❀ In a large sauté pan over medium-low heat, warm the olive oil. Add the sausage and cook slowly, breaking it up into bits with a fork, until it loses its raw color, about 5 minutes; do not allow it to brown or harden. Stir in the tomatoes and parsley. Raise the heat to medium and cook, uncovered, until the tomatoes have softened, 5–10 minutes. Stir in the cream and simmer briefly until the cream thickens slightly, about 3 minutes. Season with salt and pepper, then remove from the heat.

❀ Bring a large pot three-fourths full of salted water to a boil over high heat. Add the pasta, stir well, and cook until al dente (tender but firm to the bite), about 12 minutes or according to the package directions. While the pasta is cooking, reheat the sauce gently over low heat.

❀ Drain the pasta and return to the warm pot. Add the sauce and toss. Divide among warmed dishes and serve at once. Pass the Parmesan cheese at the table.

NUTRITIONAL ANALYSIS PER SERVING: Calories 785 (Kilojoules 3,297); Protein 31 g; Carbohydrates 74 g; Total Fat 40 g; Saturated Fat 17 g; Cholesterol 100 mg; Sodium 1,195 mg; Dietary Fiber 3 g

Spaghetti with Shrimp and Mint

PREP TIME: 30 MINUTES

COOKING TIME: 12 MINUTES

INGREDIENTS

I lb (500 g) dried spaghetti

¼ cup (2 fl oz/60 ml) olive oil

4 cloves garlic, minced

⅛ teaspoon red pepper flakes

¾ cup (6 fl oz/180 ml) dry white wine

I lb (500 g) ripe plum (Roma) tomatoes, peeled, seeded, and diced

¾ lb (375 g) large shrimp (prawns),
peeled, halved lengthwise, and
deveined

salt to taste

½ cup (¾ oz/20 g) plus 2 tablespoons
chopped fresh mint

Fresh mint imparts a lively burst of flavor to this quick seafood sauce. Add the mint at the last minute to preserve its color and refreshing character.

SERVES 4–6

❋ Bring a large pot three-fourths full of salted water to a boil over high heat. Add the pasta, stir well, and cook until al dente (tender but firm to the bite), about 12 minutes or according to the package directions.

❋ While the pasta is cooking, in a large sauté pan over medium heat, warm the olive oil. Add the garlic and red pepper flakes and sauté for 1 minute to release the garlic's fragrance. Add the wine and simmer briskly for 1–2 minutes to evaporate the alcohol. Add the tomatoes and simmer gently until the tomatoes soften slightly and render some of their juice, about 5 minutes. You don't want them to break down into a sauce. Stir in the shrimp and season with salt. Cook just until the shrimp turn pink, about 1 minute; do not overcook. Stir in the ½ cup (¾ oz/20 g) mint. Keep warm over low heat.

❋ Using tongs, transfer the spaghetti, still dripping wet, to the sauté pan. (Alternatively, drain the pasta, leaving it dripping wet. Return to the warm pot and add the sauce.) Toss the pasta well with the sauce. Divide among warmed dishes. Top with the remaining 2 tablespoons mint, dividing it evenly. Serve at once.

NUTRITIONAL ANALYSIS PER SERVING: Calories 538 (Kilojoules 2,260); Protein 24 g; Carbohydrates 74 g; Total Fat 14 g; Saturated Fat 2 g; Cholesterol 84 mg; Sodium 408 mg; Dietary Fiber 3 g

Rigatoni with Sweet Peppers

PREP TIME: 20 MINUTES

COOKING TIME: 40 MINUTES

INGREDIENTS

¼ cup (2 fl oz/60 ml) olive oil

I small yellow onion, halved and
thinly sliced

2 cloves garlic, minced

pinch of red pepper flakes

3 bell peppers (capsicums), I each
red, yellow, and green, halved,
seeded, and thinly sliced lengthwise

I tablespoon minced fresh oregano

salt to taste

20 Kalamata olives or other brine-
cured Mediterranean-style olives,
pitted and quartered

I lb (500 g) dried rigatoni or spaghetti

I cup (4 oz/125 g) grated pecorino
cheese

COOKING TIP: For a more substantial
dish, add ½ pound (250 g) fennel-
flavored Italian sausages, removed
from their casings and crumbled,
after cooking the peppers, and sauté
until the sausage is no longer pink.

Sweet bell peppers, slowly cooked, render substantial juices that transform them into a flavorful sauce. Using peppers of different colors makes the most beautiful dish, but it isn't essential.

SERVES 4–6

❀ In a large sauté pan over medium heat, warm the olive oil. Add the onion and sauté until softened, about 5 minutes. Add the garlic and red pepper flakes and sauté for 1 minute to release the garlic's fragrance. Add the bell peppers and oregano and season generously with salt. Stir to coat with the seasonings, then cover and adjust the heat so the peppers cook without burning. Cook until the peppers are soft and juicy, about 20 minutes. Stir in the olives and remove from the heat.

❀ Bring a large pot three-fourths full of salted water to a boil over high heat. Add the pasta, stir well, and cook until al dente (tender but firm to the bite), 10–12 minutes or according to the package directions. While the pasta is cooking, reheat the sauce gently over low heat.

❀ Drain the pasta and return to the warm pot. Add the sauce and toss. Divide among warmed dishes and serve at once. Pass the pecorino cheese at the table.

NUTRITIONAL ANALYSIS PER SERVING: Calories 606 (Kilojoules 2,545); Protein 17 g;
Carbohydrates 76 g; Total Fat 24 g; Saturated Fat 7 g; Cholesterol 23 mg; Sodium 1,086 mg;
Dietary Fiber 3 g

Spinach Tagliatelle with Bolognese Sauce

PREP TIME: 20 MINUTES,
    PLUS 1¼ HOURS IF MAKING
    FRESH PASTA

COOKING TIME: 4½ HOURS

INGREDIENTS

2 tablespoons olive oil

2 tablespoons unsalted butter

2 oz (60 g) pancetta, diced

½ large yellow onion, chopped

I carrot, peeled and diced

I large or 2 small celery stalks, diced

¾ lb (375 g) ground (minced) beef

½ cup (4 fl oz/125 ml) white wine

1½ cups (12 fl oz/360 ml) milk

⅛ teaspoon ground nutmeg

I can (14½ oz/455 g) whole plum
    (Roma) tomatoes, finely chopped,
    with juice

salt to taste

I lb (500 g) fresh spinach tagliatelle
    or fettuccine, homemade (page 13)
    or store-bought

½ cup (2 oz/60 g) grated Parmesan
    cheese

The secret to making a successful Bolognese sauce is long, slow cooking. There's also a surprise ingredient—milk, which adds richness and a creamy texture. Serve Bolognese sauce with dried pasta, too, such as spaghetti, penne, or medium shells.

SERVES 4–6

❀ In a large sauté pan over medium heat, warm together the olive oil, butter, and pancetta, stirring occasionally, until the pancetta renders some of its fat, about 3 minutes. Add the onion, carrot, and celery and sauté until softened, about 5 minutes. Add the beef, reduce the heat to medium-low, and cook, breaking up the meat with a wooden spoon, until the meat just loses its raw color, 3–5 minutes; do not allow to brown or harden. Add the wine, raise the heat to medium, and simmer until the wine evaporates, 2–3 minutes. Add ¾ cup (6 fl oz/180 ml) of the milk and the nutmeg. Simmer until the milk is absorbed.

❀ Add the tomatoes and season with salt. Bring to a simmer, cover partially, and adjust the heat to very low. Cook, stirring occasionally, until the sauce is thick, mellow, and tasty, about 4 hours, adding a little water if needed to keep the sauce from sticking. During the final 45 minutes, stir in the remaining ¾ cup (6 fl oz/180 ml) milk in 3 additions, allowing the sauce to absorb the milk before adding more. Taste and adjust the seasonings; keep the sauce warm over low heat.

❀ Bring a large pot three-fourths full of salted water to a boil over high heat. Add the pasta, stir well, and cook until al dente (tender but firm to the bite), about 2 minutes. Drain the pasta and return to the warm pot. Add the sauce and toss. Divide among warmed dishes. Top with a little of the Parmesan cheese. Serve at once. Pass the remaining Parmesan at the table.

NUTRITIONAL ANALYSIS PER SERVING: Calories 685 (Kilojoules 2,877); Protein 31 g; Carbohydrates 58 g; Total Fat 36 g; Saturated Fat 15 g; Cholesterol 146 mg; Sodium 925 mg; Dietary Fiber 4 g

Lemon Gelato

PREP TIME: 20 MINUTES, PLUS
8 HOURS FOR CHILLING

COOKING TIME: 8 MINUTES

INGREDIENTS

1 cup (8 fl oz/250 ml) half-and-half
(half cream)

1 cup (8 fl oz/250 ml) heavy (double)
cream

3 lemons

¾ cup (6 oz/185 g) sugar

6 egg yolks

1 cup (8 fl oz/250 ml) crème fraîche
or heavy (double) cream

The brisk, refreshing taste of lemon is always welcome after a pasta meal. In this velvety ice cream, crème fraîche contributes richness and a flavor reminiscent of cheesecake. Look for crème fraîche in good cheese shops and specialty-food stores. Serve the gelato with thin, crisp cookies.

MAKES ABOUT 1½ QT (1.5 L); SERVES 12

❀ In a nonaluminum saucepan, combine the half-and-half and cream. Using a vegetable peeler, remove the zest of 1 lemon in long strips. Add to the cream mixture. Place over medium heat and bring just to a simmer.

❀ Meanwhile, grate the zest from the remaining 2 lemons. In a food processor, combine the sugar and grated lemon zest and process until well mixed. In a bowl, combine the egg yolks and lemon sugar. Whisk until pale and smooth. Slowly whisk in the hot cream, then return the mixture to the saucepan and place over medium-low heat. Cook, stirring constantly with a wooden spoon, until the mixture visibly thickens and coats the spoon, about 4 minutes. Do not allow it to boil or it will curdle.

❀ Remove from the heat and stir for 1 minute. Let cool for 15 minutes, then whisk in the crème fraîche or cream. Cover and chill thoroughly, about 8 hours.

❀ Strain the mixture into an ice-cream maker and freeze according to the manufacturer's directions.

❀ To serve, scoop the gelato into serving dishes.

NUTRITIONAL ANALYSIS PER SERVING: Calories 253 (Kilojoules 1,063); Protein 3 g; Carbohydrates 17 g; Total Fat 20 ; Saturated Fat 11 g; Cholesterol 158 mg; Sodium 33 mg; Dietary Fiber 0

Panna Cotta with Strawberries

PREP TIME: 30 MINUTES, PLUS
8 HOURS FOR CHILLING

COOKING TIME: 5 MINUTES

INGREDIENTS

FOR THE CREAM

½ cup (4 fl oz/125 ml) milk

1 envelope (¼ oz/7 g) unflavored
gelatin

4 cups (32 fl oz/1 l) heavy (double)
cream

¾ cup (6 oz/185 g) sugar

1 piece vanilla bean (pod), 2 inches
(5 cm) long

3 tablespoons light rum

FOR THE FRUIT

2 pt (1 lb/500 g) strawberries or
other berries, hulled if necessary

¼ cup (2 oz/60 g) sugar, or to taste

This extravagantly rich, quivery cream dessert, literally "cooked cream," is the perfect companion to summer fruit. Serve on individual dessert plates, surrounded by lightly sweetened ripe berries. A small portion is completely satisfying.

SERVES 12

❈ To make the cream, place the milk in a small bowl and sprinkle the gelatin over the top. Let stand for 5 minutes to soften. Meanwhile, in a saucepan, combine the heavy cream and sugar. Split the vanilla bean in half lengthwise. Using the tip of a knife, scrape the seeds into the cream mixture. Add the pod halves to the mixture as well. Place over medium heat and stir until the cream just begins to simmer. Remove from the heat. Add the gelatin-milk mixture and stir to dissolve completely. Let cool for 10 minutes, then stir in the rum. Scoop out and discard the vanilla bean. Divide the mixture among twelve ½-cup (4–fl oz/125-ml) custard cups. Cover and refrigerate for 8 hours until set.

❈ About 1 hour before serving, prepare the fruit: In a large bowl, combine half of the strawberries with the sugar and crush with a fork. Slice the remaining berries and add to the bowl. Toss to combine, cover, and chill.

❈ To unmold the creams, set each custard cup in warm water to reach about halfway up the sides. Let stand for about 20 seconds. Remove from the water, wipe dry, then invert a serving plate over the cup and invert the serving plate and cup together. Shake gently until the cream comes loose. If it doesn't come loose easily, run a small knife around the inside edge of the cup to loosen the cream, then invert again.

❈ Spoon the berries around the unmolded creams, dividing them evenly. Serve at once.

NUTRITIONAL ANALYSIS PER SERVING: Calories 375 (Kilojoules 1,575); Protein 3 g; Carbohydrates 24 g; Total Fat 30 g; Saturated Fat 18 g; Cholesterol 110 mg; Sodium 37 mg; Dietary Fiber 1 g

Coffee Granita

PREP TIME: 30 MINUTES, PLUS
3 HOURS FOR CHILLING

INGREDIENTS

4 cups (32 fl oz/1 l) hot, strong
brewed coffee

¾ cup (6 oz/185 g) sugar, plus sugar
to taste

¾ cup (6 fl oz/180 ml) heavy (double)
cream

brandy to taste

sweetened cocoa to taste

COOKING TIP: Use strongly brewed
coffee so the flavor will come
through when the granita is frozen.
Although any roast can be used, an
Italian or espresso roast will deliver
the most authentic taste.

Made with seasonal fruit juice or, as here, with strong coffee,
flavored ices are popular all over Italy. In warm weather, a light
chilled dessert such as this one makes a particularly appealing
finale to a pasta meal.

SERVES 6

❋ In a pitcher or bowl, combine the coffee and the ¼ cup (6 oz/185 g)
sugar and stir until the sugar dissolves. Pour the mixture into a 9-by-13-
inch (23-by-33-cm) glass baking dish or other shallow container. Place in
the freezer. When the mixture starts to get icy around the edges, after
about 1 hour, use a spoon to stir and break up the ice crystals. Return to
the freezer. From that point, stir well every 15 minutes until the mixture
forms fine, firm, icy flakes, 2–2½ hours longer.

❋ In a bowl, using an electric mixer or a whisk, whip the cream until
soft peaks form. Beat in sugar and brandy to taste.

❋ To serve, scoop the coffee ice into serving dishes. Top with the whipped
cream, dividing it evenly. Lightly dust each serving with cocoa.

NUTRITIONAL ANALYSIS PER SERVING: Calories 215 (Kilojoules 903); Protein 1 g;
Carbohydrates 30 g; Total Fat 11 g; Saturated Fat 7 g; Cholesterol 41 mg; Sodium 15 mg;
Dietary Fiber 0

Pears Poached in Red Wine

PREP TIME: 30 MINUTES, PLUS
8 HOURS FOR CHILLING

COOKING TIME: 45 MINUTES

INGREDIENTS

2 cups (16 fl oz/500 ml) light, fruity
    red wine

2 cups (16 fl oz/500 ml) water

1 cup (8 oz/250 g) sugar

8 lemon zest strips

6 firm pears, preferably Bartlett
    (Williams') or Bosc

lemon juice to taste

After chilling in the wine syrup, the pears are a regal deep burgundy. Don't worry if they are pale after you poach them; they will absorb more color as they stand in the syrup. For best results, use a young, light, fruity red wine. These pretty pears make a fine dessert for a large dinner party, as you can poach them a day ahead.

SERVES 12

❁ In a saucepan just large enough to hold the pears in a single layer, combine the wine, water, sugar, and lemon zest. Place over medium heat and bring to a simmer, stirring to dissolve the sugar.

❁ Meanwhile, peel the pears, leaving the stems attached. Add to the saucepan. Cut a round of parchment (baking) paper to fit just inside the saucepan and position over the pears. Adjust the heat to maintain a gentle simmer. Cook for 15 minutes, then lift the parchment and turn the pears in the poaching liquid so they cook evenly. Replace the parchment and continue cooking until the pears are just tender when pierced (they will continue to cook as they cool), 10–15 minutes longer. Using a slotted spoon, transfer the pears to a deep bowl or baking dish.

❁ Raise the heat to high and cook the poaching liquid until reduced to 2 cups (16 fl oz/500 ml). Remove from the heat and let cool. Taste and add a little lemon juice if needed to freshen the syrup. Pour over the pears. Cover and refrigerate for 8 hours, turning the pears occasionally in the syrup to color them a deep red all over.

❁ To serve, cut the pears in half lengthwise. Remove the core from each half with a melon baller or a sharp spoon. Put the halves, cut sides down, on a cutting board and thinly slice lengthwise, leaving the slices attached at the narrow end. Using a spatula, transfer each pear half to an individual plate, maintaining the shape of the pear half. Press lightly on the slices to fan them. Strain the poaching syrup to remove the zest strips. Spoon some of the poaching syrup around the pears and serve.

NUTRITIONAL ANALYSIS PER SERVING: Calories 117 (Kilojoules 491); Protein 0; Carbohydrates 30 g; Total Fat 0; Saturated Fat 0; Cholesterol 0; Sodium 2 mg; Dietary Fiber 2 g

Mixed Fruit Salad

PREP TIME: 30 MINUTES, PLUS
4 HOURS FOR CHILLING

INGREDIENTS

1 cup (8 fl oz/250 ml) strained fresh
  orange juice

¼ cup (2 fl oz/60 ml) strained fresh
  lemon juice

½ cup (4 oz/125 g) sugar

3–4 tablespoons brandy or kirsch

½ lb (250 g) seedless red grapes,
  stemmed

½ cantaloupe, seeded, peeled, and
  diced

1 apple, peeled, cored, and diced

2 bananas, peeled, halved lengthwise,
  and thickly sliced

3 kiwifruits, peeled, halved lengthwise, and cut lengthwise into
  wedges

This refreshing Italian *macedonia di frutta* can accommodate
almost any seasonal fruits, although strawberries tend to get
mushy if marinated too long. Use the recipe as a guideline,
aiming for a variety of textures and colors.

SERVES 6

❁ In a large nonaluminum bowl, combine the orange and lemon juices,
sugar, and brandy or kirsch to taste. Stir to dissolve the sugar.

❁ Add the grapes, cantaloupe, apple, bananas, and kiwifruits. Stir to
coat with the juices. Cover and refrigerate for 4–6 hours to allow the
flavors to blend.

❁ Spoon into serving dishes and serve chilled.

NUTRITIONAL ANALYSIS PER SERVING: Calories 228 (Kilojoules 958); Protein 2 g;
Carbohydrates 52 g; Total Fat 1 g; Saturated Fat 0; Cholesterol 0; Sodium 8 mg;
Dietary Fiber 3 g

GLOSSARY

ANCHOVY FILLETS

Beloved throughout Italy, these tiny relatives of the sardine are preserved by salting and are then most commonly available packed in olive oil. The sharp-flavored, briny anchovy not only is enjoyed in its own right, but also takes on the role of a seasoning similar to that of salt in some regional pasta sauces.

ARUGULA

Found as a wild plant in its native Mediterranean, including many regions of Italy, and in other sunny climes, this green has small, elongated, multiple-lobed leaves that are enjoyed for their slightly bitter, peppery flavor.

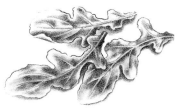

Cultivated arugula is found in well-stocked food stores, greengrocers, and farmers' markets. The cultivated variety tends to be milder and more tender. Also known as rocket and, in Italian, as *rucola*.

ASPARAGUS

Since the days of ancient Rome, Italians have grown and prized asparagus. The best is reputed to come from Ravenna, on the country's northeastern coast, and it was lauded in the writings of the Roman epigrammatist Martial almost two millennia ago. The budding tips of the asparagus stalks, trimmed in lengths of 2–5 inches (5–13 cm) depending upon size, are the vegetable's most tender part and make a particularly delicate addition to pasta dishes.

BELL PEPPERS

Although they originated in the New World, these sweet-fleshed, bell-shaped peppers, also known as capsicums, have long been a standard item in Italian kitchens. They are most commonly found in their unripened,

sharper-tasting green form, but ripened red or golden yellow varieties are sold in markets with increasing frequency. The latter, more colorful specimens add even sweeter flavor to dishes. Look, too, for the elongated, more slender varieties known as Italian sweet peppers.

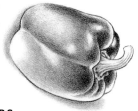

BREAD CRUMBS

Fresh and dried bread crumbs are used in Italian kitchens to add body to meatballs and in fillings for antipasti and fresh pastas. To make bread crumbs, trim away the crusts from ½ pound (250 g) fresh French- or Italian-style white bread (but not sourdough). Put the bread in a food processor and process to make soft fresh crumbs. To dry the fresh crumbs, spread them on a baking sheet and bake in a preheated 325°F (165°C) oven until dry, about 15 minutes. Let the crumbs cool, then process again until fine; return to the oven to bake until lightly colored, stirring once or twice, about 15 minutes.

EQUIPMENT

FOOD MILL
This hand-cranked mill efficiently purées tomatoes for pasta sauces by forcing them through its conical grinding disk, which also sieves out their skins and seeds. Some models have fixed disks; others come with changeable medium and fine disks for coarser or smoother puréeing.

PASTA POT
Any pot large enough to comfortably hold 5–6 quarts (5–6 l) of water is suitable for cooking 1 lb (500 g) of pasta. Cooks who cook pasta frequently, however, may find a specially made pasta pot convenient. Built with its own strainer insert, it allows the pasta to be lifted out and drained in one easy motion.

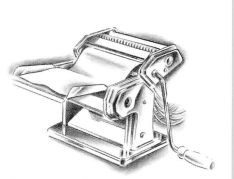

PASTA MACHINE
The classic Italian device for making pasta at home is a hand-cranked stainless-steel machine that passes fresh pasta dough between a pair of flat rollers which can be adjusted to the desired thickness. For flat cuts, the pasta sheet can then be passed through the cutting rollers (as above), which cuts the sheet into long strands.

BRESAOLA

A specialty of Lombardy in northern Italy, this cured meat is made by air-drying and aging lean, tender beef for 2 months.

BROCCOLI RABE

Not a type of broccoli at all, although it bears a resemblance, broccoli rabe—sometimes spelled broccoli raab and also referred to by the Italian *rapini*—is more closely related to the turnip.

CHEESES

The regions of Italy produce scores of different cheeses, many of which find their way into classic pasta dishes. Those used in this book include:

FONTINA

A cow's milk cheese with a firm, creamy texture and a delicate, slightly nutty flavor. The best fontina is produced in the Aosta Valley, or Val d'Aosta, of northwestern Italy.

GORGONZOLA DOLCELATTE

The milder varieties of this creamy, tangy blue-veined cheese from the town of Gorgonzola near Milan are labeled "dolcelatte," literally "sweet milk."

MOZZARELLA

This rindless white cheese has a mild flavor and soft texture. Mozzarella made in the traditional way from water buffalo's milk may be found fresh, floating in water, in well-stocked food stores and Italian delicatessens. More widely available is cow's milk mozzarella, sold both in water and packaged. Packaged products are drier and less flavorful.

Available from late spring to midautumn, the slightly bitter greens have a nutlike flavor. Both the leaves and the tender stems are generally cooked by rapid sautéing, braising, or boiling and enjoyed on their own or in pasta sauces.

CAPERS

These unopened flower buds of a bush that grows wild in the Mediterranean are pickled in salt, or a mixture of vinegar and salt, and are used whole or chopped as a piquant flavoring or garnish. Some of the best capers are salt-packed ones from Sicily, found in well-stocked food stores and Italian delicatessens; they should be soaked in cold

PARMESAN

Aged for at least two years until it has a hard, firm texture, a thick crust, and a full, sharp, salty flavor, this cow's milk cheese from the area of Parma is most often used as a seasoning, grated over pasta. Buy Parmesan in block form, to grate fresh as needed. The finest variety, designated Parmigiano-Reggiano®, is made only from midspring to midautumn, then aged for at least 14 months.

PECORINO

The term pecorino applies throughout Italy to any cheese made from sheep's milk, but it refers most often to the aged variety known as pecorino romano, which is produced in the region of Rome and used as a grating cheese like Parmesan. Look, as well, for varieties of softer, fresher young pecorino cheeses such as Toscanello and Manchego.

RICOTTA

This light-textured, very mild cheese is produced from whey left over from making other cheeses. Sheep's milk is traditionally used, although today cow's milk ricotta is more common.

water for about 15 minutes and then rinsed well before use.

EGGPLANT

Also known as aubergines, eggplants are time-honored staples of the Italian kitchen. This vegetable-fruit comes in many shapes, sizes, and even colors, although deep purple is the most familiar skin color. Italian cooks generally make use of the large, bulbous variety sometimes descriptively referred to as the globe eggplant (below). They also cook varieties known as *signorine,* "young ladies," which resemble Asian eggplants, being smaller and more slender, with a milder flavor.

FENNEL SEEDS

These small, crescent-shaped seeds come from a plant related to the bulb vegetable of the same name and share with it a mild anise flavor. Fennel seeds are a popular seasoning in Italian sausages; they also complement seafood, particularly stronger-flavored, more oily fish.

GARLIC

Prized in Italy since ancient times for its pungent, highly aromatic taste, garlic is an indispensable part of many classic pastas, particularly in partnership with olive oil or tomatoes in dishes from the country's southerly regions. For the best flavor, buy whole, firm heads of dry garlic, separating individual cloves from the head as you need them. Do not buy more than you will use in 1 to 2 weeks.

HERBS

Herbs add extra dimensions of flavor to many classic pasta dishes. To store fresh herbs, refrigerate them, either with their stem ends in a glass of water or wrapped in damp paper towels inside a plastic bag.

BASIL

This spicy-sweet, tender-leafed herb goes especially well with tomatoes.

OREGANO

Also known as wild marjoram, oregano has a spicy, aromatic flavor that pairs well with tomatoes and other vegetables.

PARSLEY, FLAT-LEAF

Also known as Italian parsley, this variety of the widely popular fresh herb, native to southern Europe, has a more pronounced flavor than its curly cousin, making it preferable as a seasoning.

SAGE

The slightly musty taste of this pungent herb complements fresh or cured pork, lamb, veal, and poultry.

THYME

An ancient herb of the eastern Mediterranean, thyme has a clean, bright, delicate taste that marries well with poultry, tomatoes, and such sauces as béchamel.

NUTMEG

The hard pit of the fruit of the nutmeg tree, this popular sweet spice was first introduced into Italy around the 12th century. It adds subtle flavor to fillings for fresh pasta, to the béchamel sauce layered in lasagna, and even to some traditional recipes for bolognese sauce. Nutmeg may be bought already ground, but the fullest flavor comes from freshly grating whole nutmeg. Small nutmeg graters are available in kitchen-supply stores for this purpose.

OLIVE OIL

The ripened fruit of the olive tree is pressed and filtered to produce an aromatic, flavorful oil that has long been favored in Mediterranean kitchens and is now enjoyed throughout the world. **Extra-virgin olive oil** is the highest grade of oil extracted on the first pressing without use of heat or chemicals. It has a distinctively fruity flavor and a color that varies depending upon the variety of olive pressed. It is used primarily to contribute character to dressings or marinades or as a condiment. Products labeled **pure olive oil** have undergone further filtering to eliminate much of their character; being less aromatic and flavorful, they are better suited to general cooking purposes.

OLIVES

Whether they are used as a featured ingredient, a garnish, or part of an antipasto platter, olives make a piquant addition to classic pasta meals. Both underripe green olives and ripe black olives may be cured using various combinations of salt, brines, oils, vinegars, and seasonings to yield a wide range of results. Well-stocked food stores and delicatessens generally carry good selections, sold either in bottles or loose by weight. **Mediterranean-style black olives** are cured in brine and packed in olive oil. Brine-cured **Kalamata olives** from Greece, by contrast, come packed in vinegar.

To pit an olive, use a small, sharp knife to slit or halve it, then pop the pit out. Alternatively, a special kitchen tool known as an olive pitter grips an olive and, with a squeeze of its handle, pushes out the pit.

PANCETTA

A specialty of the Emilia-Romagna region in northern Italy, and used throughout the country, this unsmoked bacon is cured with salt and pepper. It is sold either flat or rolled up into a sausage shape, to be sliced and used to add a rich undertone to pasta sauces and fillings.

PINE NUTS

Also known by their Italian name, *pinoli*, these small, ivory nuts are the seeds extracted from the cone of a variety of pine that grows in the Mediterranean region. They are enjoyed for their rich, pleasantly resinous taste, and may be used whole as an ingredient or a garnish or ground to lend body to sauces, particularly the classic pesto sauce of Genoa.

PORCINI MUSHROOMS

The Italian name for these wild brown-capped mushrooms (which are also known by the French *cèpes*) means "little pigs"—an apt description for their plump forms. Prized for their tender texture and rich flavor, porcini are found fresh in spring and autumn. During the rest of the year, dried porcini (below) are sold in Italian delicatessens and specialty-food stores and are a popular flavoring for pasta sauces and fillings.

PROSCIUTTO

The intense flavor and deep pink hue of this Italian raw ham, a specialty of Parma, result from first feeding pigs a diet of whey left over from the production of Parmesan cheese, then curing the hams by dry-salting for 1 month and, finally, air-drying them in cool curing sheds for 6 months or longer. Seek out authentic prosciutto di Parma for the recipes in this book. The unique qualities of prosciutto are best appreciated in tissue-thin slices. Prosciutto may be eaten raw as an antipasto, on its own or with vegetables or fruits, or it may be chopped or julienned to flavor pasta sauces and fillings.

RADICCHIO

This burgundy red member of the chicory family, a specialty of Treviso in northern Italy, is enjoyed for its vivid color, crisp texture, and refreshingly bitter taste, which together have won it the popular nickname King of Salads. The heads come in two basic shapes, round and tapered. Radicchio is, indeed, used raw in salads as well as appetizers, and is also frequently cooked, usually by grilling. Also known as red chicory.

RED PEPPER FLAKES

These coarsely crushed flakes and whole seeds of dried red chiles are added to many tomato- or olive oil–based pasta sauces to contribute a touch of moderately hot flavor. The flakes are sold in the spice section of most food stores, or dried chiles can be crushed at home with a mortar and pestle or briefly processed in an electric spice grinder.

SAUSAGE, HOT ITALIAN

Italian delicatessens and well-stocked foods stores sell fresh sausages made in the style of southern Italy, using ground (minced) pork, salt, pepper, red pepper flakes, and fennel seeds. For pasta dishes, bulk sausage meat is preferable; links may also be used, however, by slitting open and discarding the casings.

SEMOLINA FLOUR

A fairly coarse wheat flour ground from hard durum wheat. In Italy, semolina flour is preferred for the manufacture of dried pasta. It is also used to dust the surface on which freshly made pasta is held.

SHALLOTS

Enjoyed in Italy for many centuries, these members of the onion family have paper-thin brown skin that encloses pale, purple-tinged flesh. The mild flavor of shallots is appreciated in classic antipasti and pasta dishes.

SHRIMP

At home in the waters that hug Italy's coastline, shrimp (prawns) figure in many classic pasta dishes. When shrimp are prepared at home, their shells are usually peeled away and their long intestinal tracts are removed before cooking.

To peel and devein fresh shrimp, first use your thumbs to split open the thin shell between the two rows of legs along the concave side, pulling it away. Then, using a small knife, make a shallow slit along the shrimp's back, cutting just deeply enough to expose the usually dark, veinlike intestinal tract. With the tip of the knife or your fingers, lift up and pull it out, discarding it.

SWISS CHARD

This member of the cabbage family, similar in flavor to spinach, has dark green leaves and crisp white or red stems. Both leaves and stems are used in antipasti, soups, and pasta sauces. Also known as chard or silverbeet.

TOMATOES, PLUM

Roughly the size and shape of an egg, this tomato, also known as the Roma, has a high proportion of meaty flesh to juice and is well suited for use in pasta sauces. The Roma is a reliable choice for good tomato flavor and texture when other varieties of sun-ripened tomatoes are unavailable. It is also the type used most often for canned tomatoes, which are themselves an ingredient in many classic pasta sauces. When buying canned tomatoes, look for Italian brands whose labels indicate they contain the San Marzano variety of plum tomato.

To peel a fresh tomato, use a small, sharp knife to cut out its core, then immerse it in boiling water for about 20 seconds. Transfer the tomato to a bowl of ice water. The skins will peel off easily, either using your fingertips alone or with the assistance of the knife.

To seed a tomato, cut it in half horizontally and squeeze to force out the seed sacs.

TUNA, CANNED IN OLIVE OIL

While many brands of tuna fish are packed in water or vegetable oil, canned tuna from Italy is packed in olive oil, giving it richer flavor that is appealing in classic pasta dishes. Much of the canned tuna produced in Italy comes from Sicily, where fishing and canning are important industries.

VINEGARS, WINE

The word *vinegar* literally means "sour wine," describing what results when certain strains of yeast cause wine to ferment for a second time, turning it sharply acidic. The best-quality wine vinegars begin with good-quality wine. Red wine vinegar, like the wine from which it is made, has a more robust flavor than vinegar produced from white wine.

INDEX

ACKNOWLEDGMENTS

The publishers would like to thank the following people and associations for their generous assistance and support in producing this book: Desne Border, Ken DellaPenta, Jennifer Hanson, Hill Nutrition Associates, Lisa Lee, and Cecily Upton.

The following kindly lent props for photography: Fillamento, Williams-Sonoma, and Pottery Barn, San Francisco, CA, and Jane Timberlake of A-1 Products. We would like to thank Pavlina Eccless for generously sharing her lovely home with us for our location setting. The photographer would like to thank Chromeworks and ProCamera, San Francisco, CA, and FUJI Film for their generous support of this project. Special acknowledgment goes to Daniel Yearwood for the beautiful backgrounds and surface treatments.